EVERYDAY LIFE
IN
OLD TESTAMENT TIMES

1   Samaria: the plain of Shechem from Mount Gerizim

EVERYDAY LIFE
IN OLD TESTAMENT
TIMES

By
E. W. HEATON

Illustrated from Drawings by
MARJORIE QUENNELL

NEW YORK
CHARLES SCRIBNER'S SONS

3 5 7 9 11 13 15 17 19 B/C 20 18 16 14 12 10 8 6 4

Printed in the United States of America
Library of Congress Catalog Card Number 76-29288
ISBN 0-684-14836-6

FOR

JEREMY

AND

ANNE

WHO WILL AT LEAST LIKE THE PICTURES

PREFACE

"MANY of us", wrote Mark Rutherford in *The Revolution in Tanner's Lane,* "have felt that we would give all our books if we could but see with our own eyes how a single day was passed by a single ancient Jewish, Greek, or Roman family; how the house was opened in the morning; how the meals were prepared; what was said; how the husband, wife, and children went about their work; what clothes they wore, and what were their amusements." The present book makes no claim to have attained this ideal of intimate portraiture; it attempts, rather, the wider but less searching task of presenting a panorama of Israelite life, as ordinary families knew it, from about 1250 to 586 B.C.

I have tried to write for all who are interested in the Old Testament (except, of course, the learned), but I have had particularly in mind boys and girls in the upper forms of secondary and public schools, students in training colleges, freshmen at universities, teachers, and, not least, that admirable kind of general reader who wishes to read the Bible and who knows from experience that it is wise to consult a guide-book before venturing abroad.

To open the pages of the Old Testament is, indeed, to enter a foreign territory and its exploration is bound to be fruitless and frustrating, unless we discover by a little preliminary study what to expect, what to look for, and what kind of people we are likely to meet. We shall lose our bearings, if we read our Western civilization into the Old Testament and assume that the Israelites were exactly like ourselves except for their "Arab-type" clothes.

A guide-book, it is almost superfluous to say, can never be a substitute for the personal exploration of the scene and society it describes. In fidelity to the terms of my present brief, I have been able to do no more than hint at the reasons for reading the Old Testament at all. Even in the chapter on religious life, precisely because its subject is *everyday* religion, I have disciplined myself to deal only in the briefest possible way with the heart of the matter. Despite this reticence in the body of the book, I wish to use the opportunity afforded by this preface to repudiate the widespread assumption that the Old Testament is merely a quarry for the antiquarian, the examiner in quest of a set-book, or the examinee in search of marks. My purpose is not to provide a bolt-hole in the "background of the Bible" for those who wish to dodge its frontal attack, nor to equip the examination candidate with a packet of that unappetizing fodder which sometimes goes by the name of "Scripture Knowledge". It is possible, as a wise man once remarked, to be a wizard with a time-table, but never take a train. The information presented in the following pages is intended to deepen the understanding and kindle the imagination of those who, when they read the Old Testament, wish to get somewhere.

For any success this book may have in kindling the reader's imagination, most of the credit must go to Mrs. Quennell. An author could not hope for a more co-operative or stimulating artistic partner. It is far from easy to illustrate the daily life of a people who have left scarcely any pictorial records. As Christendom is flooded with colourful but dubiously accurate "Bible pictures", we have deliberately pursued a policy (but, I hope, not erred on the side) of caution. To help redress the balance after a spate of Victorian re-creations, illustrations drawn from Egyptian and Assyrian sources have often been allowed to remain looking obviously non-Israelite. In this matter, it is sometimes possible to make a virtue of necessity, by recalling that when these foreign artists depict Israelites, we learn how they appeared to their contemporaries; and it is obvious, for example, that the Assyrian war reliefs not only provide valuable analogies for Israel's fighting men and their equipment, but actually show us what the unfortunate Israelites only too often had to contend with in everyday life.

The most acute difficulty arises in trying to discover the detailed appearance of everyday clothing. Scholars are at liberty to qualify their learned discussions of the subject with a hundred footnotes, but an artist cannot dress the Israelites in the rags and tatters of academic debate. The present state of our knowledge of this intriguing topic is summarized in the chapter on home life; otherwise, Mrs. Quennell has augmented authenticated fact with artistic discretion. From the very beginning of our work together, she has shown in it an interest, which could not have been greater, even when the series to which the book belongs was peculiarly the concern and achievement of her late husband and herself. I am very grateful to Dr. A. C. Bouquet for proposing that I should collaborate with Mrs. Quennell and hope that our joint effort may prove as useful as their *Everyday Life in New Testament Times.*

Neither the text nor the illustrations would have been possible without the staggering progress which has been made in Biblical archaeology during the course of the present century. As a novice in this highly technical sphere, I should never have consented to undertake this popular account of the life of ancient Israel, without having to hand the two learned and judicious volumes of A. G. Barrois's *Manuel d'Archéologie Biblique* and the works of the American scholar, W. F. Albright, notably, *Archaeology and the Religion of Israel* and *The Archaeology of Palestine.* I am also deeply indebted to two further American scholars. First, to Millar Burrows for his invaluable book, *What mean these Stones?* and secondly, to G. Ernest Wright for his contribution to *The Westminster Historical Atlas* and for *The Biblical Archaeologist,* of which he is co-editor. The latter is a quarterly journal published by the American Schools of Oriental Research and is undoubtedly the best way in which the average teacher and student can keep in touch with the results of recent Palestinian excavation and archaeological discussion. It may be obtained in England through B. H. Blackwell, Broad Street, Oxford. Among other books which I have used and enjoyed, pride of place must go to A. Bertholet's *A History of Hebrew Civilization* and R. H. Kennett's splendidly lucid lectures on *Ancient Hebrew Social Life and Custom.* In seeking information on the details of so many things—"Of shoes—and ships—and sealing-wax—Of cabbages—and kings", I hope that I have not grossly misinterpreted any of these authorities, nor purloined in the enthusiasm of note-taking facts and phrases which I should properly have acknowledged. For any such act of inadvertence, I sincerely apologize.

Time would fail me, if I were to try to record all my other debts, but the chief must be mentioned. Publishers who give an author the impression that his work is their only child, for whom nothing is too much trouble, deservedly win such a high reputation. Samuel Carr, Director of B. T. Batsford, Ltd., London, who first suggested my undertaking this book and who are its publishers in England, has been kindness itself, borrowing rare books for me, obtaining photographs from America and Palestine, and discussing the work as it progressed with the most encouraging enthusiasm. I am also grateful to Dr. Laurence Picken, Fellow of Jesus College, Cambridge, for augmenting and correcting my draft of the section on Hebrew music; to Mrs. Dorothea Barton for helping me with a text in German; and to Mr. C. N. L. Brooke, Fellow of Gonville and Caius College, Cambridge, for again sparing me time from his own more important work. Finally, I have received invaluable help from my wife. She has reviewed all I have written from her knowledge of a land in the Mediterranean west of Palestine and from the standpoint of an English university west of my own. This powerful combination has enabled her to remove many mistakes and much jargon. What she has allowed to pass is dedicated to our children.

The Close,   E. W. HEATON
    Salisbury

CONTENTS

13

CONTENTS

14

ACKNOWLEDGMENT

THE Author and Publishers would like to thank the following for their permission to reproduce the illustrations appearing in this book:

Aerofilms Ltd. and Ewing Galloway, for fig. 1; The Trustees of the British Museum, for figs. 3 and 28; The Commissariat General, République Libanaise, for fig. 53; Dienst voor Schone Kunsten der Gemeente, The Hague, for figs. 25, 26, 58, 59, 118 and 119; Charles F. Stevens, W. F. Albright, G. Ernest Wright and *The Biblical Archaeologist*, for figs. 120 and 121; W. W. Norton & Co. Inc., New York, for fig. 103 (from *The Rise of Music in the Ancient World* by Curt Sachs); The Oriental Institute, The University of Chicago, for figs. 4, 16, 18, 50, 61–3, 80, 104–6, 115 and 116; The Palestine Archaeological Museum, for figs. 24, 27 and 117; The Palestine Exploration Fund, for fig. 60; Palestine Institute of Archaeology, Pacific School of Religion, for fig. 17; Photo Sport, Beirut, for fig. 52; Picture Post Library, for fig. 51; The Student Christian Movement Press Ltd., for fig. 88 (from *The Teachers' Commentary*); The Trustees of the late Sir Henry S. Wellcome, for fig. 15.

LIST OF ILLUSTRATIONS

The numerals in parentheses in the text refer to the *figure numbers* of the illustrations

LIST OF ILLUSTRATIONS

LIST OF ILLUSTRATIONS

2   Map of Palestine

Chapter I

THE SETTING OF EVERYDAY LIFE

IT is far from easy for most of us to appreciate that where you lived and what your forefathers had done for generations once made a great difference to everyday life. The common culture and extensive commerce of the modern western world have changed all that. We are no longer natives of our own country or county, not to speak of our own town or village, in anything like the old sense. You can read the London *Times* in the remotest parts of Africa not very long after it has been delivered in Downing Street. You can eat New Zealand lamb in the suburbs of Manchester and Coco-Cola barges display their bright yellow paint even in Venetian canals. And, of course, the universal tentacles of the American film industry have made cowboys of us all. Cities throughout the world now greet the traveller with the same commercial grin, their faces plastered with the all-too-familiar make-up. The refrigerator has conspired with rapid transport to blur even the rhythm of the seasons; the first new potatoes and the first green peas, like all first-fruits, have lost their distinction. Only the imperious contrast between summer and winter makes itself felt in our urban routine. Most people spend their lives, so to speak, under a vast umbrella, so that the climate, once so great a challenge, has become little more than a petty inconvenience.

It would be possible to illustrate *ad nauseam* the extent to which most of us live in varying degrees of indifference to the distinctive features of our own peculiar setting. The first step towards an understanding of everyday life in Old Testament times is to appreciate that it was significantly shaped by a particular scene and a particular history. The Israelite was no citizen of the world; he was more a villager than a townsman and his small country was locked by sand and sea.

THE SCENE

It is astonishing that the world should owe so much to so small a part of it. If maps have persuaded us (as they probably

23

have) that the land of Israel was about as big as any other important country, they are arch-deceivers; for Palestine, west of the Jordan, was tiny in extent—about a fifth the size of Scotland, half the size of Belgium and little more than a third the size of Switzerland. From Land's End to John o' Groats, or, as the Hebrews put it (reversing our order), "from Dan even to Beer-sheba", the distance was less than 150 miles and across the country from the Mediterranean coast to the Jordan rift was at most just over 50 miles.

Even more astonishing than the size of Palestine is its immense diversity. To go down from Jerusalem to Jericho (like the man who fell among thieves) is to drop 3,000 feet and, within a mere 15 miles, to exchange the reasonable climate and fresh mountain air of the capital for the tropical fug of a city of palms. At the northern end of the Jordan valley, the towering heights of Mount Lebanon (6,000 feet) and Mount Hermon (9,000 feet) are for ever capped with snow(52), whereas at its southern end, the river pours into the Dead Sea, its surface 1,275 feet below the Mediterranean and its depth as much again, where thick impenetrable mists rise in stifling heat. From "this awful hollow, this bit of the infernal regions come up to the surface, this hell with the sun shining into it" (as the Dead Sea appeared to George Adam Smith), there is no outlet except by evaporation and its treacly waters, laden with chemicals, make a would-be swimmer feel like a cork.

The setting of Old Testament life was a land of violent contrasts, not only between one area and the next, but between winter and summer and night and day. Everywhere, the summer sun beats down without interruption from May to October, drying up the streams and blistering the vegetation, its heat tempered only by the morning dew and the west wind blowing in from the sea. In the winter, it can be extremely cold and the rainfall is heavy. December, January and February are the wettest months, but the "early and latter rains" are the most celebrated. The early rains of October and November break the summer drought and soften the land for ploughing; the latter rains of March and April give the crops their last chance before the dry season sets in. A short spring provides the one relief from this alternation of rain and drought and then it was that the Hebrews, like our own poets, sang of flowers and making love:

3   The Black Obelisk, showing King Jehu kneeling before the Assyrian king,
Shalmaneser III

4 The Closing Scene of Old Testament times: the Babylon
of Nebuchadrezzar
This reconstruction shows the brightly enamelled Ishtar Gate,
the royal palace (where King Jehoiachin of Judah lived in exile),
with the Hanging Gardens on its roof. The Tower of Babel may
be seen in the background on the right

> My beloved spake, and said unto me,
> Rise up, my love, my fair one, and come away.
> For, lo, the winter is past,
> The rain is over and gone;
> The flowers appear on the earth;
> The time of singing is come,
> And the voice of the turtle dove is heard in our land;
> The fig tree ripeneth her green figs,
> And the vines are in blossom,
> They give forth their fragrance
>
> (Song of Songs 2. 10–13).

This was also the great moment for the sheep and cattle which were able to enjoy for these few weeks a little fresh pasture. What little grazing the summer sun spared was blasted by the deadly Sirocco, the scorching sand-laden wind from the eastern desert, which is far and away the worst feature of the country's difficult climate.

Palestine is not a farmer's paradise, but even its stony hills can be made to grow fruit trees, and the staple agricultural products of the land have always been the olive and the vine. In Old Testament times, before the big irrigation projects which are now transforming Jewish agriculture, grain crops could be grown only in the valleys and on the coastal plain. The area called the Shephelah ("Lowland"), for example, in the foothills of the central limestone ridge west of Judah was no less valuable for its grain, than for its strategic position as a barrier against invaders. Apart from this fertile region, however, most of the rich agricultural land was in the north and especially in the valley of Jezreel, guarded by the Megiddo Pass. The prosperity of Samaria, which became the Northern Kingdom, proved to be its undoing; what it gained in wealth, it lost in stability.

Although Samaria, like Judah, its southern neighbour, was largely rugged and mountainous, broad valleys (like the one shown in our frontispiece) encouraged it to look outwards, whereas the Judean hills encouraged a spirit of detachment and became the stronghold of Israel's distinctive life, almost as immune from the invasion of foreign religion as from the invasion of foreign chariotry. The Old Testament is essentially a highland literature, the writers of which for the most part look down upon the scene and see the march of events from the vantage-point of the Judean hill-country.

27

The march of events, as we shall see in a moment, was of considerable significance in Old Testament times and, even in the Southern Kingdom, the Israelites were not simply left to inspect it from a distance. By its geographical position, Palestine was inevitably involved in the politics and trade of the great empires which rose and fell on her borders. The coast-land of the country was a bottleneck through which merchants and armies alike had to pass between Africa and Asia (see the map on p. 43). The rivalries between Egypt in the south and Assyria and Babylon in the north-east constantly brought the insignificant kingdoms of Israel into the ebb and flow of Near-Eastern imperialism. Nobody wanted Palestine, but nobody could afford to ignore her strategic importance.

Apart from the brutal impact of invading armies, the less spectacular influence of the desert in the south was always a force to be reckoned with. From that region came not only the detested Sirocco, but also the hardly less disturbing infiltration of semi-nomadic tribesmen, which in times of severe drought assumed the dimensions of a minor invasion. They brought with them a distinctive manner of life, as well as hungry mouths, and both were calculated to upset the urban security of men who were doing their best to forget that their own forefathers had once been wandering nomads.

From one direction at least, the Israelites remained un-influenced and that was from the west. The Mediterranean was not a highway but a barrier and its smooth coast-line, devoid of natural harbours, was never in our period given any ports. It is significant that there is no word for port in the Hebrew language.

The scene of Israel's everyday life made it for the most part austere and economically insecure; but the land was a world in miniature and endowed its people with that high degree of adaptability without which their subsequent history would be inconceivable.

THE PERIOD

From a strictly chronological point of view, Old Testament times stretch from Genesis to the book of Daniel, beginning with the call of Abraham and ending with the Maccabean revolt. They cover, that is to say, no less than eighteen centuries, from about 1950 B.C. to 165 B.C. Our information about the details of everyday life is more adequate for the middle of this long period than for the first and last centuries and it is a fortunate (but not entirely fortuitous) circumstance that the best documented phase of Israel's life is also the most representative and intrinsically important. This middle period begins with the Exodus from Egypt, which was the prelude to the Conquest of the Promised Land, and ends with the fall of Jerusalem, which marked the collapse of the Hebrew monarchy and the loss of political independence. It was during these years (1250–586 B.C.) that Israel came into being as a distinctive people, marked off from her neighbours and cousins by her religious foundation and calling, and developed the social, political and religious institutions, which are characteristic of the overwhelming bulk of the Old Testament writings.

After the fall of Jerusalem, most of the new developments in the customs, manners, art, architecture, religion and thought of the Jews were borrowed from the great empires of which they successively became a part—first the Persian and then the Greek. This post-exilic period was a time of great cultural expansion and reformation in Judaism and, despite the dictates of strict chronology, the study of it belongs less to Old Testament times than to the background of the New Testament. Everything after 586 B.C. falls, therefore, outside our present concern.

It is easier to decide to bring down the curtain on the fall of Jerusalem than to decide where to raise it for the beginning of our period. The Old Testament is a collection of writings produced by and for a people leading a settled existence in the towns and villages of Palestine and accepting in many everyday things the pattern established by the Canaanite inhabitants of the land before them. The religious leaders of Israel, however, constantly referred back to the period before the settlement, when their forefathers were wandering shepherds. Their especial interest lay in the religious significance of the work of Moses, but their ideal was in no sense narrowly religious. It included a conception of social custom and morality which they struggled to maintain in the midst of the more sophisticated culture of Canaan. In addition to this conscious attempt to keep alive the values of the people's nomadic past, part of the desert outlook lived on in the strong traditions of Hebrew family life. It is, therefore, impossible to understand Israel in Canaan without remembering Israel in the wilderness. The Israelites never abandoned their flocks of sheep and goats and this pastoral life may be taken to symbolize a more fundamental and far-reaching continuity of tradition.

Old Testament times, as the expression is understood in this book, is, therefore, the period from the Exodus to the Exile, that is, from about 1250 B.C. to 586 B.C. In the language of the archaeologist, we are concerned with Israel in the Iron Age. The compilers of the Old Testament have greatly assisted our understanding of these centuries by prefacing their historical account of it with a sketch (in Genesis) of the age of the Patriarchs. Similarly, we shall be wise to give a brief account of everyday life among the nomads of Israel as a curtain-raiser to our main theme. It will be found in the next chapter.

Everyday life is always too deeply rooted in ordinary human nature to change as rapidly as systems of government and lines of kings. It goes on with an imperious disregard for newspaper headlines and political crises. And yet the details of everyday life, if not its essence, are refashioned from age to age as political authority and material resources are redistributed, increased or withdrawn. It is not adequate, therefore, to view Old Testament times simply as what the cinema industry calls a "still"; it should, ideally, be presented as a "movie". For our purpose, however, it will be enough to suggest the main lines of development by passing under rapid review the nine dominant phases into which our period may be divided.

(i) *Wandering Shepherds* (2000–1300 B.C.)

The origins of any people are difficult to trace and in so far as they can be discovered are always complicated. We shall not be far wrong, however, if we think of the Hebrews at the time they entered recorded history as an element among the desert tribes which swept into the Fertile Crescent about 2000 B.C. The Fertile Crescent is the great semicircle of well-watered land stretching from Egypt to the Persian Gulf through Palestine, Syria and the Tigris-Euphrates valley, along which the main trade-routes ran (see the map on p. 43). The Amorites, as these nomadic people were called, established numerous small kingdoms throughout this area. Of the various Amorite kings, history best remembers Hammurabi of Babylon (perhaps a contemporary of Abraham), whose chief claim to fame was his Code of Law.

Not all the invading tribesmen settled down to a regular life in cities and among those who continued to live in tents on the fringe of civilization were the Hebrews. The picture of Abraham, Isaac and Jacob in Genesis shows the Patriarchs pursuing a semi-nomadic existence with their asses, sheep and goats. Some of the Hebrew shepherds found their way to the pastures of the Egyptian Delta, where they remained (according to tradition) a full four centuries. These men were to become the creative core of the people we call Israel, whose noble faith was the preparation in history for Christianity. Christianity too began as shepherds, abiding in the field, kept watch over their flock by night.

(ii) *Liberated Slaves* (about 1300–1250 B.C.)

For generations, the Hebrews prospered in Egypt and one of them—Joseph—rose to the exalted position of Prime Minister. And then, as we are told in Exodus 1. 8, "there arose a new king over Egypt, which knew not Joseph". Under Sethos I, who reigned in Egypt from 1319–1301 B.C. and is probably the Pharaoh referred to, the fortunes of the Hebrews suddenly changed for the worse. This Egyptian monarch was keen to rebuild some of his cities and seized the Hebrews as slave labour for the purpose. According to the familiar story, they were set to work in the brickyards(73). Against this degrading servitude, one of their number—Moses—rebelled. Inspired by a vision of God, which made a new man of him and earned him the title of the first of Israel's prophets, he persuaded the dejected tribesmen to risk everything in a desperate bid for freedom. The story of what followed is the great epic of Israel's literature and the historical foundation of her faith. Would that its details were as clear as its importance!

The Exodus journey appears to have begun with a march south and then there followed (by a miracle) the crossing of the Reed (not *Red*) Sea. It was the successful negotiation of this obstacle and the drowning of the pursuing Egyptian chariotry which were for ever after celebrated in the people's national songs (see Exodus 15). We do not know exactly where the Reed Sea was (perhaps at some point along the present Suez Canal), nor the exact route of the desert trek which followed. Whatever the details, Moses achieved his primary object in leading the tribes out of Egypt when, at Mount Sinai, he inaugurated a covenant between them and God, by which they pledged themselves to obey his voice and pursue his purpose. The people of Israel came into being in response to God's act of deliverance.

(iii) *Conquering Heroes* (1250–1225 B.C.)

Despite Israel's pledge at the Mountain of God, unity among the tribesmen in the exacting conditions of the desert was difficult to maintain. The cities in the south of Palestine were too heavily fortified to storm and after considerable delays Moses determined to by-pass Edom and Moab and bring his people into Transjordania. Here his task was completed and Joshua succeeded him as leader.

The enthusiasm of the book of Joshua demands, perhaps, a pinch of salt, but its account of the conquest of western Palestine has been substantially confirmed by recent archaeological excavation. After an interval of 3,000 years, Bethel, Lachish and Debir have yielded debris which clearly dates their destruction at this period. The fall of Jericho, the most dramatic of Joshua's successes (Joshua 6), remains, on the other hand, a headache to competent historians. The archaeological evidence suggests that the city was destroyed at least a century before Joshua arrived on the scene! It is possible that the city did not fall to Joshua after all, but to Hebrews, who either had never been in Egypt or had returned to Palestine years before the enslavement and liberation. The presence of friends and relations to welcome Joshua when he and his people crossed the Jordan would also help explain why the invaders managed to occupy central Palestine without, apparently, striking a blow. We may take it, then, that Joshua's task was greatly eased by the good work of an advance party. It was not, however, accomplished as completely as the historian would have us believe: "So Joshua took the whole land, according to all that the Lord spake unto Moses; and Joshua gave it for an inheritance unto Israel according to their divisions by their tribes. And the land had rest from war" (Joshua 11. 23). In fact, the conquering heroes of Israel, unaccustomed to "mechanized" warfare (see Judges 1, 19 and pp. 149–51), had to be content to occupy the hill-country and leave the lowlands and many of the fortified cities (Jerusalem, Megiddo, etc.) in the hands of the enemy.

(iv) *Amateur Citizens* (1225–1020 B.C.)

If the Israelites knew little about the art of war, they knew even less about the gentler arts of peace. Like the survivors of the devastating war in the film version of H. G. Wells's *The Shape of Things to Come*, who (if memory serves) harnessed horses to dilapidated Rolls-Royce motor-cars, the Israelites made what they could of the ruins to which they had reduced the cities of Palestine. They built their own crude homes on the remaining foundations of noblemen's houses and dignified mansions were hastily patched up to accommodate numerous families. Nevertheless, these amateur citizens were remarkably quick at learning the ropes of this new settled way of life. Although they were impoverished and unskilled, they managed to build many new towns in their first two centuries and before the end of the period appear even to have established connexions with international trade.

The new settlers, however, retained their tribal organization, with its clans and families, and their jealously guarded traditions and separate loyalties must have made anything like political unity very difficult to achieve. Some measure of common action was ensured by the central sanctuary established at Shiloh (Joshua 18. 1), but this proved inadequate as a unifying force in face of the dangers which threatened. These came from the unconquered inhabitants of the land (the "Canaanites"), from the kingdoms of Moab and Ammon across the Jordan, from the desert Midianites and their camel raiders, and, above all, from the Philistines. The Philistines were sea-people from the Greek islands, who had settled in a confederation of five cities (Gaza, Ashkelon, Ashdod, Ekron and Gath) on the coastal plain. They inflicted heavy defeats on the Israelites and even destroyed Shiloh (I Samuel 4). Under this constant external pressure, there arose a new type of leader who has given his name to this settling-in period—the age of the "judges". Such judges as Ehud, Barak, Gideon and Jephthah were not primarily legal men, but military heroes, who were thought to possess a special measure of divine power and wisdom. Thus, they were able to claim a loyalty and exercise an authority which transcended the tribal divisions. The spontaneous rise of these temporary leaders shows that the tribal organization had had its day. It could not serve in the new conditions of civilized life and the

5 Capital in the
Phoenician Style

time was ripe for Israel to copy the surrounding nations and establish a monarchy.

(v) *Royal Subjects* (1020–926 B.C.)

During the century spanned by the first three kings of Israel—Saul, David and Solomon, there was a rapid improvement in the material prosperity of the country and a corresponding deterioration in its spiritual values. The court of the neurotic Saul at Gibeah was simple enough, but under David, the monarchy got into its stride. With the conquest of the Philistines, Edomites, Moabites, Ammonites and Syrians, both the territory and the revenue of Israel were greatly increased, and the establishment of Jerusalem as capital of the kingdom helped to break down tribal loyalties and to win the allegiance of the whole population to the person of the king(16). David had dreams of organizing his people on bureaucratic lines for taxation and military service, but when he tried to take a census as a first step in this direction, the outcry was so great that he was forced to drop it.

Solomon inherited his father's fortune and the opportunity for realizing his frustrated schemes. The country was divided into twelve administrative districts and royal officers began to exact a heavy burden of taxation from the king's subjects. Over and above all this, large labour gangs were conscripted to work on grandiose building projects. Jerusalem became a show-place with its new temple, palace and government offices—

6   Phoenician Merchant Vessel

all executed in the most up-to-date Phoenician style(5). Splendid cities were built as garrisons for the king's new chariotry and as headquarters for his regular army.

Immense commercial enterprises were required to balance the Budget and it is now clearer than ever that Solomon went into Big Business. He built a merchant navy for the Red Sea traffic(6), monopolized the trade in horses and chariots between Egypt and Syria, and exploited the copper mines in the region of Ezion-geber on a scale which even

7 Ivory decoration from Ahab's palace

the commercial tycoons of the twentieth century might very well envy.

Solomon indubitably put his country on the map and even the fabulous Queen of Sheba was more than a little impressed. Had Moses been alive to comment, he would probably have said that the achievement of this century marked the beginning of the end.

(vi) *Rebellious Northerners* (926–800 B.C.)

The instability of Solomon's Forty Glorious Years was shown up in the chaos which followed his death. The kingdom which he inherited from David had been kept together only by a strong central government and the moment this was removed, it broke into its two natural divisions—*Israel* (in the north) and *Judah* (in the south).[1] For a time, Palestine was torn by civil war, to which probably the heavy fortifications recently excavated at the Judean town of Mizpah(17) bear witness. Eventually, it seems that Judah, weakened by a devastating invasion from Egypt, gave up the unequal struggle and agreed to play second fiddle to the Northern Kingdom.

The interest of the ninth century in Palestine is almost entirely concentrated in the upstart Northern Kingdom, established by Jeroboam I. The writers of the books of Kings, who were men of the south, treat him as the culprit "who made Israel to sin", largely because he set up Dan and Bethel as religious centres

[1] Although the name "Israel" is used to describe the Northern Kingdom, it is also used more generally to describe the whole people. Throughout this book Israel, Israelite and Hebrew are used as general, rather than technical, descriptions.

to rival Jerusalem. The turbulent spirit which brought him to the throne also removed from it, by assassination, the four kings who followed, so that it was not until the reigns of Omri and Ahab that the new kingdom enjoyed any stable government. The prosperity of the Omri dynasty has come to light in the excavations of the northern capital at Samaria (see pp. 208 ff.) and its fame is proved by the Assyrian records which refer to Israel as the "House of Omri" long after it had been overthrown. It was brought to a violent end about 845 B.C. in a military *coup d'état* plotted by an army general called Jehu. With incredible ferocity, Jehu and his supporters massacred the whole of Ahab's family. Among those supporters were the prophets Elijah and Elisha—for reasons which the social history of the next century makes abundantly clear.

(vii) *Plutocrats, Paupers and Prisoners* (800–721 B.C.)

During the first part of the eighth century, both the Northern Kingdom (under Jeroboam II) and the Southern Kingdom (under Uzziah) enjoyed a post-war boom. The great powers on the borders were quiet and nothing stood in the way of commercial expansion and material prosperity. So much is evident from the books of Amos, Hosea, Isaiah and Micah, which give us first-hand evidence of the internal state of society. These prophets make it clear that the newly acquired wealth was not so much benefiting the many as corrupting the few. Money talks, and its power in Israel was concentrated in the hands of a new class of plutocrats, who cared not a fig for justice and even less for the traditional faith of their fathers. As early as the middle of the ninth century, the struggle of Naboth to protect his ancestral property from Ahab's Phoenician wife, the grasping Jezebel (I Kings 21), indicated the plight of the peasant proprietor and the championship of his cause by Elijah gave a foretaste of the prophets' protest against the overthrowing of Israel's deep sense of social equality. That protest reached its climax in the preaching of Amos, who exposed the callous greed of the new-rich, the pathetic fate of the small farmers who were driven to the moneylender, debt and ultimate slavery, the collapse of justice by bribery and corruption, and the foulness of the rites which masqueraded as religion among the fashionable set. Amos believed that the people of the north would not go unpunished for their moral

8   Assyrians bringing in Prisoners and Booty.
Notice some of their victims impaled on the hill

and religious degeneration, and the march of events confirmed his conviction.

The power of Assyria, to whom Jehu had already paid tribute (3), revived about the time of Jeroboam II's death and in 732 B.C. Israel's ally, Damascus, was overrun and absorbed into the Assyrian Empire. The Northern Kingdom escaped the same fate by a hair's breadth and for ten precarious years retained a nominal independence. The king then refused to pay his tribute and, in 721 B.C., after a two years' siege, Samaria fell to the Assyrian armies. Over 27,000 prisoners were deported and the Northern Kingdom came to an end(8).

(viii) *Subservient Tradesmen* (721–600 B.C.)

Judah (with whom alone our story now continues) never ran to the extremes of her late lamented sister of the north. The excavation of southern towns reveals a more conservative tradition both in religious and social affairs. There does not seem to have been, for example, quite so notorious a cleavage between rich and poor as in the more prosperous Samaria and (to judge by the houses and textile industry of Debir) a solid middle class, organized into trade guilds, formed the backbone of the population. It is clear, however, that the tradesmen of Judah were denied any comfortable sense of security during the century which preceded the collapse of their State.

.Twenty years after the end of the Northern Kingdom, Hezekiah of Judah thought that he saw a chance of ridding his people of the intolerably heavy tribute demanded by Assyria and so (in alliance with Babylon and Egypt) revolted against

37

the overlord. Anticipating the possibility of a siege of Jerusalem, he commissioned his royal engineers to build the Siloam Tunnel to protect the city's water-supply (see pp.137–9). Sure enough, the Assyrian army did invade Palestine in 701 B.C. Forty-six cities were stormed and taken and Jerusalem itself was saved only at the cost of a crippling payment.

Judah, now reduced to a strip of territory about 100 miles long and less than 50 miles wide and to the status of a weak Assyrian dependency, was ruled by Manasseh for the first half of the seventh century. His loyalty to his Assyrian masters saved the country politically, but it came near to ruining its religion. When Josiah succeeded to the throne about 640 B.C., the outlook for Judah took on new hope. The power of Assyria was on the wane and after 625 B.C. rapidly collapsed. The new king was encouraged, therefore, to assert himself and his enterprise in the circumstances was inevitably a mixture of politics and religion. He purged the country of its corrupt local sanctuaries, making Jerusalem the one legitimate centre for worship, and attempted (with some success) to gain political and religious control over the mixed population of the Assyrian province, which had once been the northern kingdom of Israel. He lived long enough to see the final collapse of the Assyrian Empire under pressure from the rising power of Babylon and died in the battle which was (so to speak) Assyria's funeral.

The change-over from Assyrian to Babylonian supremacy soon proved to be no better for Judah than a transfer from the frying-pan into the fire.

(ix) *Exiles* (598–586 B.C.)

Life in Judah during these last twelve years must have been unbearable. Despite the unswerving and courageous insistence of Jeremiah that the country should accept Babylonian rule, its imbecile king Jehoiakim listened to the nationalistic tub-thumping of his court circle and in 598 B.C. openly rebelled. He died (or was murdered) before Nebuchadrezzar's army reached Jerusalem and it was left to his son and successor, the eighteen-year-old Jehoiachin, to suffer the humiliation of surrender and exile. A great number of Judah's leading citizens were deported to Babylon with him.

Those who were left struggled on under the vacillating rule of Zedekiah, the young king's uncle. Jerusalem was only half-populated and other cities were too stricken even to repair their shattered houses and broken defences. This nightmare period of living and partly living lasted only a few years, for in 589 B.C., Zedekiah, as though determined to seal his country's doom, conspired with Egypt and again repudiated the rule of Babylon. This stupid act of defiance hastened the end. The armies of Nebuchadrezzar advanced and razed to the ground one fortified city after another in southern Judah. The famous military correspondence, known as the Lachish Letters, which was found twenty years ago in and around a burnt-out guard-room, gives first-hand evidence of the chaos and strain in that city on the eve of its destruction. The turn of Jerusalem soon followed and in 586 B.C., after a hopeless resistance lasting eighteen months, it was finally taken. In the second deportation, thousands of Judeans were taken as exiles to Babylon(4), leaving behind them a ruined temple and the last vestiges of their political independence.

Chapter II

NOMADIC LIFE

O RTHODOX Israelite parents never tired of recalling the early days of their people and telling their children how, once upon a time, before ever their ancestors thought of settling down in cities and becoming farmers and traders, their great-great-great grandfather was a nomadic Aramean (Deuteronomy 26. 5), wandering in the wild open spaces, where he pastured his sheep and goats. No doubt many of the younger generation failed to share their elders' enthusiasm for those good old days and scarcely concealed their preference for the more comfortable life of the city, where at least you could be more certain of a square meal and even now and then a few odd luxuries. But even the younger generation were interested to hear the rest of the tale, recounting how, after a period of enslavement in Egypt, their forefathers were safely led through the wilderness by Moses and finally brought by Joshua into the Promised Land. They did not so much like being reminded of Moses (who was, as they said, an austere man), but at least they recognized that he had done well in instigating the conquest of Palestine.

Even in Palestine, however, it was far from easy wholly to forget Moses and the wilderness wanderings, since the desert—the home of the nomad—forced itself on everybody's attention and pushed menacingly to the very gates of the cities. This was especially the case in the hill-country of Judah, where the so-called fields which surrounded the fortified walls were for the most part nothing but patches of rugged moorland, strewn with boulders. The meagre scrub which managed to grow there seemed only to provide cover for marauding bears and lions, which the Old Testament calls rather too mildly, "the beasts of the field"(9). Even from the Mount of Olives just outside Jerusalem, the terrifying Wilderness of Judah (aptly called Jeshimon, or, Devastation) could be seen by anybody who looked towards the south-east, and from the hills of Tekoa, only a few miles farther south, it was quite inescapable. It is not surprising, therefore, that the prophet Amos, who came

40

9   The species of Lion formerly found in Palestine
(*From ivory carvings of the ninth century* B.C.)

from Tekoa, should have reacted to the lush living of Samaria
with something of the rigorous insight of his forebear Moses.
Moses himself had once abandoned the flesh-pots of Egypt
and spent a good part of his youth in the desert with a nomadic
Midianite tribe. From his own roof-top, Amos had been able
to gaze eastwards across the 15 miles of barren Judean wilderness
before it suddenly plunged headlong into the valley of the
Dead Sea. Beyond this torrid chasm, there was the abrupt rise
of the mountains of Moab to catch the eye. Not many miles
south, Amos could have reached the desert, inhabited now only
by a few Arab Bedouin, who brave the heat and sand-laden
blast of the summer and the intense cold which the winter
brings.

Israel's connexion with the life of the desert was not, therefore, simply a piece of past history to be remembered or
forgotten according to choice; it was a significant part of the
everyday experience of a fair proportion of the population.
Even after Israel had been occupying her cities and sharing the
civilization of the Near East for many centuries, the desert
still asserted its influence. Apart from the indirect influence of
the unchanging scene from the lofty table-land of Judah, the
memory of the people's nomadic origin was constantly refreshed
by the incursion of men from the desert. It is not to be expected
that the nomadic tribes, who from time to time crossed the
frontier between "the desert and the sown", should have found
a significant place in the historical record of the Old Testament
(kings are news, but not shepherds!), but there can be no doubt
that the population was frequently rejuvenated by transfusions
of nomadic blood. It is seriously conjectured, for example,
that the revolt of Jehu against the corrupt dynasty of Omri
owed much to the influence of nomads recently arrived from

41

the desert and it is actually on record that one Jonadab, the son of Rechab, was intimately concerned in it (II Kings 10. 1–28). The extent to which the Rechabite tradition was nomadic may be judged from the summary statement of it which was given in the time of Jeremiah:

> We have obeyed the voice of Jonadab the son of Rechab our father in all that he charged us, to drink no wine all our days . . . nor to build houses for us to dwell in: neither have we vineyard, nor field, nor seed: but we have dwelt in tents, and have obeyed, and done according to all that Jonadab our father commanded us (Jeremiah 35. 8–10).

No doubt the Rechabites were a minority group of extremists, but the fact that tradition associates them with the prophets suggests that they cannot be lightly dismissed as lone voices crying in the wilderness. Their nomadic ideal sprang from the desert setting of Israel's original and authentic faith and it was a vital element in the teaching of her religious leaders.

It would, of course, be idle to pretend that the average city-dwelling Israelite enthusiastically shared this ideal. To say that fierce Bedouin blood flowed in the veins of every Hebrew would be as romantic and inaccurate as to say that every inhabitant of the British Isles was by nature an intrepid seafarer. To most ordinary men of Old Testament times, the desert was clearly an "evil place . . . no place of seed, or of figs, or of vines, or of pomegranates; neither is there any water to drink" (Numbers 20. 5); it was regarded as an enemy which threatened their settled way of life—a no-man's-land inhabited by serpents, scorpions, wild asses, jackals and wild cats, and overrun by nettles, thorns and thistles. The contrast between the "howling wilderness" and the seemingly luxurious land of Palestine is very well expressed in the Song of Moses (see Deuteronomy 32. 7–14). This is one of a number of Old Testament passages which suggest that at least some of the forefathers of Israel passed directly from nomadic to agricultural life without the intervening period of the sojourn and enslavement in Egypt. It is clear that Israel's nomadic origin is more complicated than the straightforward account from Genesis to Joshua suggests. Fortunately, recent archaeological discoveries have brought us nearer to an understanding of what really happened.

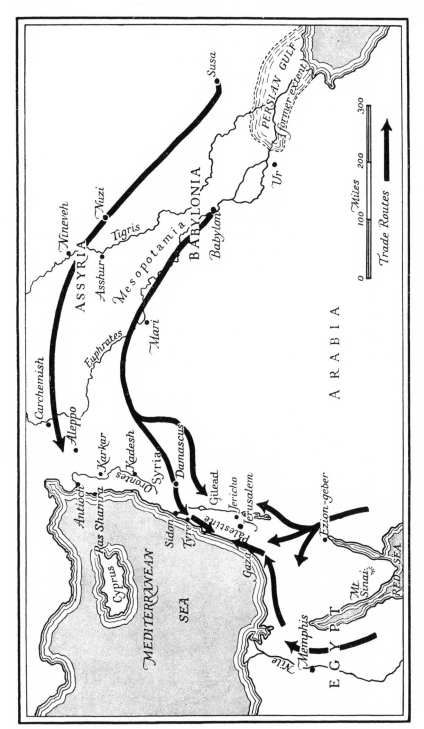

10 The Fertile Crescent and its Lines of Communication

According to Genesis 11. 31, Abraham migrated with his father from Ur of the Chaldees on the Persian Gulf to Haran in north-west Mesopotamia and from Haran, he moved into Palestine, "the land of Canaan" (Genesis 12. 5). The kind of civilization which existed in north-west Mesopotamia at the time of Abraham (?1900–1750 B.C.) has been brought to light by remarkable discoveries at Mari, the capital of an important State on the Euphrates some 200 miles south of Haran (see map on p. 43). The interest of finding the huge palace of the king (with its chapel, scribe's chambers and luxurious bathroom) was eclipsed by the unearthing of the royal archives, consisting of 20,000 clay tablets dealing with business and diplomatic affairs. These documents show that by the eighteenth century B.C. Amorite tribes (akin to that of Abraham) had settled in this region and the *place* names which they contain actually correspond to the *personal* names of some of the members of Abraham's family (Serug, Nahor, Terah). The Mari tablets also make it clear that some of the nomadic tribes had not yet settled down and were still making themselves a nuisance in the cities. One of the tablets is a letter written by the king on this subject:

> The Benjaminites have taken to raiding. Once they made a raid, and took many sheep. I sent auxiliary troops against them, who slew their chieftain. Not one of them got away, and all the sheep which they had taken were returned. However, a second time they made a raid, and took sheep, and I sent auxiliary troops who caught them and slew their chieftain, and brought back the sheep they had taken. Yet a third time they did likewise . . .[1]

The interest of this letter is not in the possibility of a connexion between these Benjaminites and the later Israelite tribe, but in the illustration it affords of the constant threat to civilized communities from nomadic groups in the age of the Patriarchs.

More extensive illustration of the presence of nomadic bandits in western Asia (including Palestine) between 2000 and 1200 B.C. comes from tablets of the period, which refer to people called *Habiru* (or, Apiru). It will be recalled that Abraham is called "the Hebrew" (Genesis 14. 13) and it is noticeable that in the Old Testament this term is most used in the records of the Patriarchal age. Although it would be

[1] Quoted by G. E. Mendenhall, *The Biblical Archaeologist*, February 1948.

going beyond the evidence to say that *Habiru* and Hebrew are identical in meaning, there can be little doubt that the names are related. They probably began as a term of contempt applied by the settled communities to the wandering bandits which haunted them throughout this period.

The Habiru, it now appears, sometimes settled down sufficiently to become mercenary troops, hired labourers, and even slaves in the households of the sedentary population. For example, among the Nuzi tablets, from an Assyrian city inhabited in the fifteenth century B.C. by a non-Semitic people which the Old Testament calls Horites or Hivites, there is one which reads: "Sin-Balti, a Habiru woman, caused herself to enter the house of Tehiptilla in servitude. If Sin-Balti breaks the contract and goes into another house, Tehiptilla may pluck out Sin-Balti's eyes and sell her for a price." For the most part, however, the Habiru preferred to wander in raiding bands on the desert fringes of civilization. It is extremely likely that the Hebrews made up one of the elements of this nomadic group. Our newly discovered information certainly increases our respect for the general reliability of the stories of Abraham and his family and we may say that the traditions of Israel's origin in north-west Mesopotamia have been remarkably confirmed.

The story of Genesis goes on to tell how eventually Israel migrated from Palestine to Egypt and settled in the fertile eastern part of the Nile Delta called "the land of Goshen" (a phrase, incidentally, used in various parts of England for good farmland even today). Here they lived for four centuries in peace and prosperity until they were reduced to slavery, when "there arose a new king over Egypt, who knew not Joseph". Israel's great epic then relates how they were delivered by Moses, who led them through the wilderness to the borders of the Promised Land.

The historical setting of this migration to Egypt again forces on our attention the nomadic background of Israel's life. We know that about 1720 B.C., Egypt was invaded by tribes from Syria and Palestine who were successful in seizing and controlling the country until 1550 B.C., when they were expelled. It was about the beginning of this period that Joseph rose to prominence in Egypt and became Prime Minister (Genesis 41. 41f.). The Egyptians referred to these invaders by the contemptuous term *Hyksos*, which has been taken to mean "princes of the shepherds", and all the evidence indicates that they were Semitic people closely related to the shepherd patriarchs of Israel. When the main body of the Hyksos were expelled from Egypt in 1550 B.C., perhaps some of the Hebrews were reduced to slavery, while others returned to Palestine. It is at least clear that when the Israelites invaded Palestine after the Exodus, they met with friends as well as enemies. These friends evidently occupied central Palestine (which, to judge by our historical records, needed no conquering). Whether they had come out of Egypt with the Hyksos or whether they were Habiru who had never left Palestine, we do not know; but they must have been semi-nomads of Hebrew stock.

The growing mass of archaeological evidence which shows that when the tribesmen under Joshua destroyed the Canaanite fortresses they *reoccupied them almost immediately* demands that we should define the nature of Israelite nomadic life with a little more precision. The full-blooded Bedouin is in no great hurry to settle down and if we think of the early Hebrews as wild men from the desert, we are almost certainly on the wrong track.

The true Bedouin relies on his camel; it takes him across vast stretches of desert, where sheep and goats could not possibly exist; it supplies him with milk and in emergencies with food. This tough kind of life does not at all square with the picture of the Patriarchs given in Genesis. Consider, for example, the explanation given by Jacob to Esau of his reasons for wanting to bring up the rear as they journeyed:

> My lord knoweth that the children are tender, and that the flocks and herds with me give suck: and if they overdrive them one day, all the flocks will die. Let my lord, I pray thee, pass over before his servant: and I will lead on softly, according to the pace of the cattle that is before me and according to the pace of the children (Genesis 33. 13f.).

This is far from camel nomadism. Indeed, many distinguished scholars now take the view that the camel was not domesticated until after the patriarchal period and affirm that the Hebrews of Genesis used only asses (e.g. Genesis 22. 3). It is reckoned that an ass-nomad can cover only about twenty miles a day and this radically affects our mental picture of the kind of life lived by the early Hebrews. Instead of thinking of them as undertaking long treks over blistering sand, we must visualize small clans making regular seasonal movements, with their asses, sheep and goats, between the desert regions of the south (where they spent the late winter and early spring) and the hill-country of central Palestine, to which they were driven by the summer heat, and, where, so to speak, each clan had its own regular beat. During their seasons in the hill-country, the early Hebrews lived on the fringe of settled communities (like Mamre, Beersheba, Bethel, Shechem and Dothan) with whom, no doubt, they were fairly closely associated. Even in the desert region of the Negeb (the "parched" land in the south), where Abraham is said to have lived for a period (Genesis 13. 1; 20. 1), it is now reported that there were in his time, "a considerable number of permanent, agricultural villages with stone houses".[1]

The stories of Abraham, Isaac and Jacob reveal a kind of life which is properly called *semi*-nomadic—half-way between that of the desert Bedouin and the settled farmer. No true desert ranger (even in his wildest dreams) would have imagined himself to be binding sheaves in the field as did Joseph (Genesis 37. 7) and, from the strict Bedouin point of view, it would be no less strange to hear of Isaac sowing (Genesis 26. 12) and Reuben in the harvest field (Genesis 30. 14). On the other hand, bickering over precious wells (Genesis 21. 25 ff.) is characteristic of nomadic life and so are the migrations to fertile regions in time of famine (Genesis 12. 10). The journeys of Abraham and Jacob's sons are illuminated by Egyptian documents which show how Semitic nomads were allowed to enter the country under strict supervision during time of famine. The famous painting in the tomb of an Egyptian nobleman at Beni Hasan from about 1900 B.C., depicting a nomadic chieftain with his clan, is the nearest approximation we shall ever get to a portrait of the Patriarchs as they went down to Egypt on these occasions (11). Our first reaction to the scene is that the men and women do not look in the very least wild or "primitive". Next, we notice that their baggage and children are carried not on camels but asses. But it is their clothes and equipment which provide the greatest interest.

The artist has been careful to make a distinction between the white linen loin-cloths of the Egyptians and the ornate embroidered garments of the Asiatics. The shorts of the little boy

[1] Nelson Glueck, *The Biblical Archaeologist*, February 1955.

11   A Nomadic Clan entering Egypt in the age

following the first ass are red; the men's "kilts" (for clearly they are not simple loin-cloths) are blue and red striped, except those of the lyre-player and bowman behind the second ass, which are red and white. A number of the men and all the women wear an embroidered tunic fastened over one shoulder; the feminine version comes well below the knee. The men have sandals on their feet, but the women a kind of boot. We may take it for granted that the artist has flattered his subjects and represented them in their very best clothes. Among other fascinating details are the skin water bottle strapped to the back of the lyre-player, the bow and quiver of the archer, the javelins, the heavy throw-sticks, the saddle-cloths of the asses and the lyre. The puzzling objects carried by the asses have been identified by Professor W. F. Albright as two pairs of goat-skin bellows and the conclusion has been drawn that these semi-nomads were travelling metal workers—forerunners of the tinkers of a later period. While it is possible that some of the Hebrew clans eked out a living like modern gipsies, it would be dangerous to assume that this splendid Egyptian picture is in all respects representative. In particular, the two soft-eyed gazelles probably owe their inclusion more to a convention of Egyptian art than to a knowledge of the flocks characteristic of the semi-nomad.

The early Hebrews were essentially keepers of sheep and goats and their shepherd's ways, always regarded as superior to those of the farmer, remained a feature of everyday life throughout Old Testament times. The prophet Amos and King David were both taken "from following the flock" and both were men of Judah.

Judaea, indeed (wrote George Adam Smith), offers as good ground as there is in all the East for observing the grandeur of the

of the Patriarchs (*From a contemporary painting*)

shepherd's character. On the boundless Eastern pasture, so different from the narrow meadows and dyked hillsides with which we are familiar, the shepherd is indispensable. With us sheep are often left to themselves; but I do not remember ever to have seen in the East a flock of sheep without a shepherd. In such a landscape as Judaea, where a day's pasture is thinly scattered over an unfenced tract of country, covered with delusive paths, still frequented by wild beasts, and rolling off into the desert, the man and his character are indispensable. On some high moor, across which at night the hyenas howl, when you meet him, sleepless, far-sighted, weather-beaten, armed, leaning on his staff, and looking out over his scattered sheep, every one of them on his heart, you understand why the shepherd of Judaea sprang to the front in his people's history; why they gave his name to their king, and made him the symbol of Providence; why Christ took him as the type of self-sacrifice.[1]

We shall appreciate the greatness of Israel's shepherds only if we resist the temptation to romanticize their work. When, for example, we read the prophet's metaphorical description of God—"He shall feed his flock like a shepherd, he shall gather the lambs in his arm, and carry them in his bosom" (Isaiah 40. 11), it is essential to remember that (unlike their stained-glass representations) lambs could be heavy and dirty. Though the shepherd be never so gentle, his life was rough and exhausting. Jacob's description neatly picks out its salient features:

This twenty years have I been with thee; thy ewes and thy she-goats have not cast their young, and the rams of thy flocks have I not eaten. That which was torn of beasts I brought not unto thee; I bare the loss of it; of my hand didst thou require it, whether stolen by day or stolen by night. Thus I was; in the day the drought consumed me, and the frost by night; and my sleep fled from mine eyes (Genesis 31. 38–40).

[1] *The Historical Geography of the Holy Land*, pp. 301f.

12   A Hebrew Shepherd leading his sheep

If a shepherd managed to rescue only "two legs, or a piece of an ear" (Amos 3. 12) from a marauding lion or bear, he could still prove to his master that his sheep had in fact been worried and not cashed with a passing clan. As flocks were so often tended by slaves, as well as by members of the owner's family, authentic evidence was necessary and was even demanded by an official enactment in the law (Exodus 22. 13). The hazards of the shepherd's calling sufficiently explain why, in addition to his long staff, he always carried a stout wooden club about three feet long(12).

As we have seen, a day's work for a shepherd lasted twenty-four hours. He counted his sheep each morning and evening as they passed under his staff on leaving and re-entering the rough stone enclosures on the hillsides which did duty as folds. In gathering his flock for the night, he neither used nor needed to use our familiar sheep dog. His method, though it has become familiar, remains astonishing:

> Sometimes [to quote from George Adam Smith's great book again] we enjoyed our noonday rest beside one of those Judaean wells, to which three or four shepherds come down with their flocks. The flocks mixed with each other, and we wondered how each shepherd would get his own again. But . . . the shepherds one

50

by one went up different sides of the valley, and each called out his peculiar call; and the sheep of each drew out of the crowd to their own shepherd, and the flocks passed away as orderly as they came.

The Palestinian shepherd who calls and *leads* his sheep is immortalized by the description of the Good Shepherd in the tenth chapter of St. John's gospel.

These remarkably intelligent animals were valued chiefly for their wool, which was sheared in spring at the end of the lambing season. As we should expect, the harvest of fleeces was *the* day of the year for the shepherd community and was celebrated accordingly (I Samuel 25. 4ff.). Ezekiel's use of shepherd's language in his condemnation of the corrupt leaders of the nation—"Ye eat the fat, and ye clothe you with the wool" (34. 3) is a reminder of the Israelites' liking for mutton. Indeed, the court of Solomon consumed sheep at the rate of a hundred a day! Of all the carcase, the fat tail of the big-tailed Palestinian sheep (which weighed anything up to 15 pounds) was the most highly prized. This was the dainty dish which Samuel's cook set before the king, according to the correct translation of I Samuel 9. 24: "And the cook took up the thigh and the fat tail and set it before Saul." Otherwise, a shepherd's food, at least as long as he led a semi-nomadic life, must have been meagre and extremely dull.

The goats which often ran with the sheep supplied milk, but above all they produced the hair which the women spun and wove in narrow strips on their primitive looms(56). From this crude cloth were made the black tents in which all nomads lived(13). Obviously, they varied in size according to the wealth of the owner, but even the more modest tent had two compartments—one for the men and entertaining (the "parlour") and one for the women, children and cooking (the "kitchen"). Occasionally, women enjoyed the luxury of a separate tent. It is impossible to be certain, but the nomad's tent was probably like a small version of the kind of long, low, refreshment tent you find at agricultural shows and cricket matches in England, closed on three sides and open at the front and subdivided into compartments by hangings. The tent cloth was erected on poles with the familiar arrangement of guy ropes and pegs. So much at least may be gathered from the archaic metaphor of Isaiah 54. 2: "Enlarge the place of thy tent, and let them

13   A Camp in the Desert

stretch forth the curtains of thine habitations; spare not: lengthen thy cords, and strengthen thy stakes." It is strange how the tent life of the nomadic shepherd continued to exercise its fascination (as this reference proves) at the very end of Old Testament times. The antique form of the priestly tabernacle, which remained half tent and half temple (Exodus 26 and 36), is more easily accounted for in terms of Israel's conservative religious tradition.

14 A pottery Water Bottle

It would be pompous to describe the nomad's camping equipment as furniture. Obviously, no large pieces could be carried on his asses (although, poor beasts, they were made to take big enough loads); everything had to be portable. Instead of chairs, he used straw mats or carpets and for a table, a skin was stretched on the ground. This could be gathered up by a cord ringed round its edges into a useful bag, a method we have just rediscovered for the plastic sheets we take to the beach. Perhaps the most precious piece of equipment was the water bottle, of which the importance is graphically illustrated in the story of Hagar (Genesis 21. 14–19). It was made of the whole skin of a kid or goat and carried on the back(11). Milk was also stored in it and drunk sour or churned into oily butter. The delightful story of Abraham, who entertained angels unawares (Genesis 18), providing water for their feet and a feast of meal cakes, veal, butter and milk, illustrates that generous hospitality to strangers which is typical of life in the desert.

Such hospitality is part of the nomads' deep-seated sense of being (for good or ill) members of a close-knit family, whose very existence in a land of scanty vegetation, meagre water supplies, wild beasts and enemy raiders, depended on the full sharing by all of a common life. The tribal structure of Israel was born in the desert, although the division of the people into twelve tribes (with subdivisions of clans and families) belongs to a more systematic and less realistic arrangement on a geographical basis made after the conquest of Palestine. The essence of tribal life is to be found in the conviction of all its members that they share a common blood, which, incidentally, helps explain why the Old Testament contains so many tedious genealogies. This tribal solidarity found one of its most characteristic expressions in the practice of avenging the blood of any of its members who were killed by enemies. The story of Gideon's vengeance on the two kings of Midian shows an approach to the custom which is astonishingly matter-of-fact: "And he said, They were my brethren, the sons of my mother: as the Lord liveth, if ye had saved them alive, I would not slay you" (Judges 8. 19). Blood vengeance in tribal society is not a way of teaching the enemy his lesson, nor is it primarily a confused emotional response of the tit-for-tat kind. In the most literal sense of the words, blood vengeance is the way of getting your own back, of healing the breach which has been made in the life of your family. That is why no compensation is good enough.

The solidarity and honour of the tribe were vested in its chief. It is significant, however, that in Hebrew there is no word for chief. He was clearly no autocrat, empowered to issue orders, for nomadic life was nothing if not democratic. An old Arabic Bedouin poem admirably expressed the mutual dependence of the chief and the members of his tribe in a metaphor drawn from the poles and pegs of their tents:

> A folk that hath no chiefs must soon decay,
> And chiefs it hath not when the mob bears sway.
> Only with poles the tent is reared at last,
> And poles it hath not, save the pegs hold fast.
> But when the pegs and poles are once combined
> Then stands accomplished that which was designed.[1]

This nomadic ideal survived the settlement of Israel in Palestine and the establishment of the Hebrew monarchy. It set fixed bounds to the despotic tendencies of Israel's kings and through her great prophets has entered and continues to influence the thinking of Christendom.

[1] Quoted by A. Bertholet (trans. A. K. Dallas), *A History of Hebrew Civilization*, p. 122.

Chapter III

TOWN LIFE

THE typical city of Old Testament times looked like a large castle set on the crown of a hill. Its solid stone-and-brick walls followed the irregular outlines of the mound on which it was built, and so gave an impression very different from the rather box-like fortresses of neighbouring lands. The reconstruction of Mizpah(17) well suggests the appearance of an ordinary provincial city in the early days of the monarchy and the "air view" of Lachish(15) illustrates the kind of city with which the contemporaries of Jeremiah were familiar. A glance at the reconstructed Ishtar Gate of Babylon(4) is enough to show how much more systematically Mesopotamian architects set about their planning and building.

Although fortified cities like Mizpah and Lachish were so distinctive a feature of Palestine in Old Testament times, they owed relatively little to the architects of Israel. Their style was borrowed from the Canaanites whom the Israelites drove out at the Conquest. Indeed, the grandeur of the Canaanite walled cities was one of the things which struck terror into the hearts of the semi-nomadic invaders, to whom it was reported that "The people is greater and taller than we; the cities are great and fenced up to heaven" (Deuteronomy 1. 28). Perhaps it was partly the massive masonry of the Canaanite fortresses which encouraged the unsophisticated tent-dwellers to believe that in earlier times veritable giants had walked the earth.

The Israelites took over from the Canaanites not only their architectural style, but many of the cities which they had built. A great number of the cities which were occupied during the period of the monarchy already had a history stretching back many centuries. By systematic excavation, it has been established that these fortresses were constructed for the petty kings who ruled and squabbled in Palestine long before the Israelites arrived on the scene(80), and that their coming brought about a marked decline in all the amenities of civilized life. Indeed, the Israelite invasion of Palestine has been compared to the barbarian invasions of the Roman Empire and the Arab

55

invasion of the Byzantine Empire in later centuries. The Hebrews, on their arrival from the wilderness, were completely ignorant of the art of building, as their patching and improvization abundantly prove. The new walls they erected were jerry-built by comparison with those they replaced and their houses to begin with were crude and unworthy of the old foundations on which they were usually built. Large residences previously owned by the Canaanite nobility were divided up and reduced to what we should call "flats", housing more than one family (and, perhaps, even their cattle). The decline in the standard of pottery tells the same sorry story. But perhaps the story is not so sorry after all, if it is borne in mind that part of this drop in material culture may be accounted for by the Israelites' love of freedom. The splendid cities of Canaan were built by slave labour and that was something which men from the desert would not tolerate. They preferred their tradition of tribal democracy to urban amenities purchased at so great a cost.

It is difficult to be as greatly impressed as the Israelites with the size of these cities. On the contrary, it comes as rather a shock to learn how minute they actually were. Jerusalem, for example, was only 13 acres in area, Megiddo the same and Debir a mere $7\frac{1}{2}$—figures which begin to have some meaning, when it is remembered that 640 acres are needed to cover a square mile. The imagination boggles when you compare them with English cities like Birmingham (51,147 acres), Liverpool (27,255) or Bristol (26,345). The population, of course, was correspondingly small. It is reckoned, for example, that a fairly typical Judean town like Debir had about 1,000 people living within its walls, occupying between 150 and 250 houses. Only the fortifications of these minute communities forbids their being classified as villages.

To the Israelite, villages meant the collections of huts and tents which were dotted about the grazing land round the city walls. The size of these extra-mural communities fluctuated very greatly. During periods of peace and security, the city population overflowed and, thus, fairly large "suburbs" were established. It is not surprising that little direct evidence has survived of such expansions, although at Mizpah, for example, grain pits, cisterns and houses have been unearthed outside the city's defences. The double wall at Lachish(15) illustrates

15 The City of Lachish, with its two fortified walls, double gate, and governor's palace

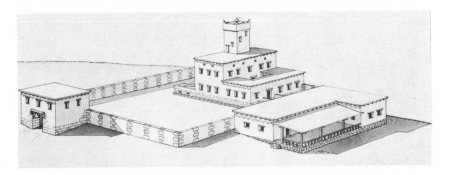

16 An Outpost of David's Government at Megiddo

17 The Fortifications of Mizpah—a typical Israelite provincial town eight miles north of Jerusalem

FORTIFICATIONS

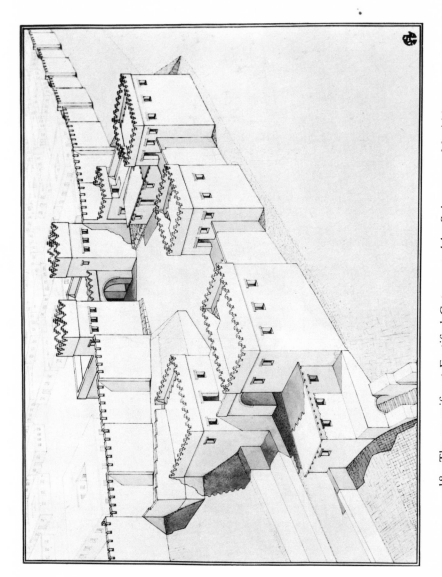

18 The magnificent Fortified Gate erected by Solomon at Megiddo

how attempts were made to cope with the situation when the city became too congested. The fluctuation of population between the city and its suburban villages was not limited to alternating periods of war and peace; it happened regularly every year. During the summer months, the few permanent villagers were joined by the vast bulk of the city-dwellers, who abandoned their fortress to work in the fields and graze their cattle in the surrounding countryside. This alternation between summer and winter quarters still goes on among Mediterranean peoples today. For about two-thirds of the year, then, Hebrew cities wore a forlorn and deserted appearance, with only a handful of regular soldiers and civil servants left to keep life ticking over within the walls. One can imagine what a tremendous thrill the coming of spring must have been to families who had spent the winter months cooped up in damp and overcrowded slums and what a joy it must have been to leave the filth and congestion of the streets, just when the wild anemones and cyclamen were coming into flower.

The sites of Old Testament cities were originally chosen for their strategic importance in warfare and the Israelites followed the example of their predecessors in this as in other matters. For example, Lachish, one of the largest cities of ancient Judah, was refurbished and equipped by Solomon's son as one of a string of fortresses to protect the frontier from the neighbouring Philistines. Megiddo, in the northern plain of Esdraelon, which guarded the main highway between Asia and Africa, was developed into an important centre of one of Solomon's new administrative districts and a military stronghold. Mizpah, again, about eight miles north of Jerusalem, was built as a frontier town during the wretched little wars between the Northern and Southern Kingdoms.

While military considerations determined the general locality of these cities, the particular spot chosen depended (at least in the early part of the period) on the water-supply. However, the Israelites soon learned to line their cisterns with waterproof lime plaster. This was a great step forward, because it enabled them to collect and store rain water and so to build at some distance from springs and streams. Lachish, for example, did not rely on any spring in the immediate neighbourhood and many of the houses had their own cisterns dug in the ground or excavated out of the solid rock. Attempts were made to build drains to feed such cisterns, but much of the water found its own way into the reservoir from the roofs and the streets. The filth it took with it is better not mentioned.

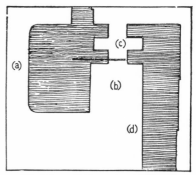

19   Plan of the gate at Mizpah

The most impressive feature of all Israelite cities, as you ascended the rubble road up the rampart, was the fortified gate. The great east gate of Mizpah is a splendid example and because it brings to life so many Old Testament scenes is worth pausing over. It was formed by an overlapping of the ends of the walls of the city, so that a "corridor" about thirty feet wide was left in between (19). This arrangement had a double advantage. First, it meant that anybody trying to enter the city was forced to turn left round the end tower of the outside wall (a) and, therefore, to expose his right side (unprotected by a shield) to the guards stationed on the walls (d). Secondly, it made an admirable market-place. Along the walls of the "corridor" (b), long stone benches had been built, from which, it is easy to imagine, many a dispute was settled, many a bargain made and many a story told. At the inner end of this "corridor", there were two sets of gates built about thirty feet apart, forming a small courtyard (c). On each side of this court was a guard-room, equipped with a stone seat for the man on duty.

The extraordinarily impressive gate of Megiddo is another example too good to pass over (18). A small double gate (built round four piers) brought you first into a fortified and paved courtyard. It is difficult to imagine a better spot for a "forum". If you were approaching the city on foot, you could avoid the long chariot road and take a short-cut up the mound which led to steps by the outer gate (shown in the bottom left-hand corner of the photograph). Before you reached the city proper, you still had to pass through the colossal main gate, which had no less than four doorways. The first of these was about fourteen feet wide and fitted with two heavy hard cypress doors, hung on stone sockets. We know that city gates were locked at night (Joshua 2. 5) and it is fairly certain that a strong metal bar, fitting into slots, was used.

What archaeological reconstructions and architectural descriptions can never convey is the teeming activity of the gate in Old Testament times. It was the hub around which the whole life of the city revolved, being for the population in general what the flat roof was for the individual householder—the place where you met your friends, gossiped and caught up with the news of the day. Behind the hubbub of ordinary social activity, there were deep-seated sacred associations which made the gate a very special place. The Canaanite custom of laying the foundations of the city gate with a human sacrifice had not altogether been forgotten, and its special significance is suggested by the fact that when Jerusalem was rebuilt by Nehemiah after the Exile, the priests "purified the people, *and the gates*".

The sacred nature of the gate, added to the practical consideration that it was the only open space in the city where people could assemble, made it the seat of local government and justice. When David, for example, was persuaded to address his people at a time of crisis, "the king arose, and sat in the gate . . . and all the people came before the king" (II Samuel 19. 8). It was at the gate that the elders, who were at once the City Council and the Justices of the Peace, held their regular assemblies. The book of Job gives a vivid picture of such a gathering, with the hangers-on listening in the background:

> When I went forth to the gate unto the city,
> When I prepared my seat in the street,
> The young men saw me and hid themselves,
> And the aged rose up and stood;
> The princes refrained talking,
> And laid their hand on their mouth;
> The voice of the nobles was hushed . . .
> Unto me men gave ear, and waited,
> And kept silence for my counsel.
> After my words they spake not again (29. 7–10, 21 f.).

There is another vivid little scene in the fourth chapter of the book of Ruth, which shows how the elders settled one of their cases. This particular dispute was highly technical and concerned the law of inheritance; but the real interest of the account lies in the picture it gives of the ten elders sitting gravely on their benches, the two disputants standing before them, and a mixed crowd of citizens and loafers on the fringe of the assembly until, eventually, they were drawn in as witnesses.

To describe the crowd which thronged the gate in the morning and evening would be to catalogue all the sorts and conditions of men who made up Israelite society. Here, you would find the wretched beggars squatting in the dust; the peddlers touting for trade and singing their songs; the labourers waiting to be hired for the day; the scribe offering to write your letters; the stranger seeking a bed for the night; the tradesmen and shoppers haggling over prices; and, perhaps, above the din, an eccentric-looking prophet trying to proclaim the word of the Lord.

In the bigger cities, shopkeepers established themselves in their own special quarters, as they do still in the East and as they did in mediaeval England—hence such familiar names as Baker Street and Butchers' Row. The prophet Jeremiah, for example, was given daily "a loaf of bread out of the bakers' street" (37. 21). Such quarters were hardly shopping centres so much as strings of untidy bazaars, whose owners snoozed in the background, until they were roused by a potential customer or by the cries which greeted the upskittling of the rickety stands on which they displayed their goods at the edge of the street. The monotony of the bazaars was broken from time to time by the arrival of a caravan of merchants, who were greeted as enthusiastically as the mail boat paying her monthly visit to an isolated island today. Some of these merchants came from distant lands, bringing luxuries like ivory, spices and perfumes, and they were treated with great respect. Occasionally it was arranged that foreign traders should have a special quarter of the city set apart for their use, like the exchange agreed between Damascus and Samaria (I Kings 20. 34). Usually, however, travelling merchants displayed their wares in the gate, where they met the local producers anxious to sell their oil, their textiles, their leather goods or whatever speciality the particular city had to offer (20).

20 A Merchant weighing Gold
(*see p.* 190)

The fact that at a later period one of the gates of Jerusalem was called the "Dung Gate" brings to mind the filth of these open markets. As there were no squares of any kind inside the city walls (Hebrew significantly lacks a word for such open places), every day brought a large proportion of the citizens crowding into the restricted area of the gate and they left, inevitably, unimaginable litter. The mud and refuse of the streets are taken for granted by the Old Testament writers (see, for example, Isaiah 5. 25 and 10. 6) and the accumulation of broken pots, crumbled mud-bricks and household garbage, combined with the road "surface" of dust and ashes, must have made a veritable quagmire every time it rained. The stench in summer can have been little more pleasant. To understand an Israelite city, we must forget all our modern notions of sanitation and be prepared to be impressed when an excavator solemnly reports the discovery of one primitive drain. It is not surprising that the street level often rose above the ground floor of many of the houses. Some people, like Rahab of Jericho (Joshua 2), were lucky enough to have houses on the city walls, but the majority lived in buildings bordering the streets. It would be more accurate, however, to say that the streets were the spaces left between the houses—narrow alleys about seven feet wide, which wound their way round corners and up hills without rhyme or reason. The unhappy pedestrian made his way hopefully, keeping close to the walls of the houses all the time, to avoid the mud in winter and in summer the glare of the sun. The Old Testament knows nothing about walking arm in arm; if you went out with a friend, you walked in single file and not abreast. To follow a person is, therefore, to accompany him. The congestion in these alleys makes modern traffic problems pale into insignificance. It is astonishing to discover, for instance, that hardly any cities possessed even a "ring road" round the inside of the walls and there is not a trace of any planned system for taking the traffic into the city from the gates. Some cities had gates wide enough to admit two horse-drawn chariots abreast, but it is likely that most heavy vehicles had to park outside the city boundary. This is probably true of loaded camels as well, but there is no doubt that asses, horses and cattle were allowed inside the walls to make confusion worse confounded. Jeremiah tells us, incidentally, that dead asses were simply dragged along the streets and thrown outside the gate (22. 19). There were no Medical Officers of Health to worry about flies and germs.

We can only make a guess at the *noise* of the city. The men of the East are notorious for their volubility. We have it on the authority of the gospels that the Pharisees of Jesus' time liked to receive "salutations in the market-place" and the Old Testament provides evidence from an earlier period that elaborate ceremonial greetings were exchanged whenever people met. There was a right and a wrong way of performing these ceremonies and children from their earliest days were schooled in the proper etiquette. The lanes of the city rang out, however, with more strident sounds, for above the chatter of friends and the cross-talk of merchants at their bargaining, there were the cries of the hawkers. A chance quotation has rescued one of them from oblivion. It is probable that in Isaiah 55. 1—"Ho! every one that thirsteth, come ye to the waters"—there is an echo of the cry of the water-seller. At night, when the gates were shut, the noise of the city died down, only to be broken by the occasional shout of the nightwatchman and the yelping of mangy dogs scavenging in the garbage.

The spade of the archaeologist has to a small extent relieved this rather squalid picture of life in an Old Testament city. Professor Albright, for example, has reported that

> at the West Gate of Tell Beit Mirsim [Debir] we discovered that the northern part of the gate tower contained a rectangular court, entered through a wide doorway from the interior of the town. This open, lime-paved court gave access to six paved rooms, each provided with a stout door which could be barred to protect the person occupying it at night. Wall cupboards, a built-in basin for washing, and other conveniences suggested at once that this was the official guest-house of the pre-exilic Jewish town; the discovery of standard weights in it seems to prove that among the guests were merchants or tax-collectors, or both.[1]

Guest-houses have always played an important part in the life of the East and it is probable that they were to be found in most Israelite cities.

Excavations have also made it clear that most cities possessed one or two other big buildings, planned on a more lavish scale than the wretched little houses of the common people(21).

[1] *The Archaeology of Palestine*, pp. 139f.

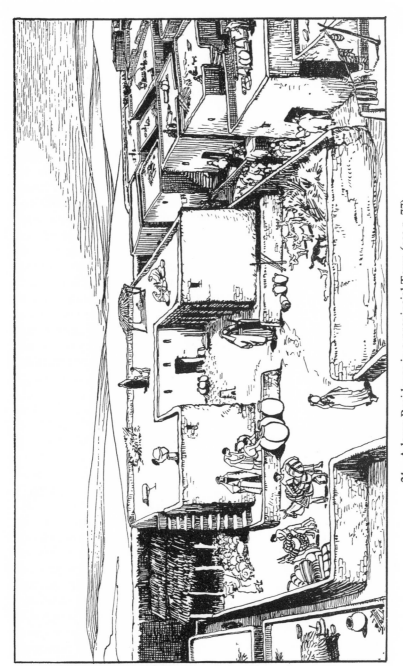

21 A large Residence in a provincial Town (*see p.* 77)

Indeed, it is an exaggeration to suggest that the latter were planned at all. At Mizpah, for example, it is evident that a large proportion of the population lived in shacks patched up from the ruins of older buildings and that they were "as a rule poorer in their masonry than those of the smallest and poorest Arab villages of today".[1] If, however, a city were fortunate enough to enjoy royal patronage, building was done on the grand scale and carefully executed with well-dressed stone. Megiddo was one such city. The splendid reconstruction shown in the photograph(106) gives a clear impression of how much was achieved. Some scholars have interpreted the foundations of the large building near the east wall of the city as being those of a temple, but it is more probable that they belonged to an official residence used either by the city governor or the military commander in charge of the nearby barracks and stables. Here, as elsewhere, the first thing which strikes the eye of a person accustomed to western architecture is the succession of flat roofs. The main building was half-timbered, built, that is to say, of stone, mud-brick and wood. It has even been established by the chemical analysis of a scrap of charred wood that cedar was used. At one corner of the building, there protrudes a solid-looking tower with outside stairs. This was evidently for the look-out man and it was well placed to cover not only the city walls but a considerable part of the surrounding countryside.

Even more impressive is Megiddo's magnificent group of stables. What the excavators found may be seen in the photograph(105). Whenever standing pillars like these have been discovered on Palestinian sites, it has been tempting to interpret them as the "standing pillars" of Israelite sanctuaries (see pp. 217f.), but there is little doubt that most of them were part of the structure of buildings—probably roof-supports. In this particular building, they also served as tie-posts for horses. Altogether, four of these stables have been excavated at Megiddo and it has been calculated that they provided accommodation for about 450 animals. Their plan is as curiously modern as their external appearance. Each stable was made up of four or five "units". Each unit was about 25 yards long and divided up the middle by a passage about 10 feet wide which was paved with a smooth limestone cement. On each

[1] C. C. McCown, *Tell en-Nasbeh*, vol. I, p. 206.

side of this passage, there was a row of stone pillars to which the horses were tied. They stood facing each other in two rows of fifteen; their stalls were cobbled to prevent slipping and each stall was equipped with a manger hewn out of a solid limestone block. The reconstruction(104) shows five of these stable units grouped together at one side of a paved courtyard with a watering-trough in the centre. The discovery of these stables demonstrates how much skilled builders could achieve in the tenth century B.C. and how faithfully Solomon's initiative has been reported in the Old Testament.

Although Solomon's wealth and commercial ambition make his Megiddo buildings somewhat exceptional, other cities also had one or two large residences of which they could boast. The reconstruction of Lachish(15) shows how it too was dominated by the governor's palace. Unfortunately, little is known about this building beyond the rather boring fact that it was constructed on a platform about 35 yards square and in this respect resembled the "Millo" erected by David in the middle of Jerusalem (II Samuel 5. 9). Alongside this large palace, there was another fair-sized building with five long parallel chambers, which, it is thought, was a granary of the kind to be found in the royal "store cities" (I Kings 9. 19).

The list of grand buildings in Israelite cities is soon exhausted and it would be misleading to make too much of them. Despite their massive defences, the urban communities of the period were essentially intimate and rural. Their citizens were not townsmen in our sense of the word. Common needs bound them to their neighbours; their work took them to the fields and vineyards for a great part of the year; and the smell of the earth and cattle was never far from their nostrils.

Chapter IV

HOME LIFE

I<small>T</small> would be impossible to exaggerate the importance of the family in Hebrew society. In the semi-nomadic days of Israel's history, the life of the family (in our sense of the word) was inevitably bound up with the life of the larger "family" of the clan and the tribe, upon which it depended for protection. When, however, the Israelites became farmers and townsmen, the larger unit was of less importance and the feeling which held it together was more difficult to maintain. Settling down in Palestine had the effect of singling out the individual family (as we now know it), based on the father's house; the tribe lost much of its meaning and its break-up was hastened by the deliberate policy of the early kings, who were determined to establish a centralized form of government for the whole country.

Although the external threats of the desert had largely disappeared in Old Testament times, the sheer struggle for existence continued and demanded a sharing of work and a family loyalty which have much to teach any society which pampers its members and encourages every man to get what he can for himself.

FAMILY RELATIONS

A modern Western European inevitably finds the internal relations of an ancient Hebrew family extraordinarily confusing. Even though memories of the Victorian Age prepare him for the large number of children, they do not prepare him for the head of the household's having two wives at the same time, so that often one half of the children were step-brothers and step-sisters to the other half. It requires little imagination to appreciate that jealousies and friction easily arose in such circumstances and one wonders how, with such explosive ingredients, the Israelite family held together at all.

The stability of the family was clearly founded on the absolute authority of the father. He ruled his wives and children as an Oriental potentate ruled his kingdom; the family

68

was his property and subject to his sovereign will. He could sell his daughters into slavery and have any disobedient children put to death. He could divorce a wife without giving any explanation and without accepting any responsibility for her maintenance. He could not, however, sell his sons, but he could and did arrange their marriages.

By the strict letter of the law, the status of the Israelite woman could hardly have been worse. She could not leave her husband, because he *owned* her, as he owned his sheep and goats; but she could be sent away by him at a moment's notice. She was exposed, moreover, to the humiliation of finding herself playing second fiddle to a new wife whom her husband had recently acquired and preferred. She was unable to inherit property and her plight in widowhood is constantly coupled in the Old Testament with that of the orphans and the poor.

Everyday life, however, was more humane than the strict letter of the law and, in fact, the lot of the Israelite woman seems rarely to have been as bad as theoretically it might have been. Women like Miriam, Deborah, Huldah and Michal (the wife of David) were not exactly downtrodden, inhibited creatures, and in the family circle it is evident that the mother as well as the father received the respect and affection of their children. Her position would scarcely satisfy a Mrs. Pankhurst and the militant feminists of the twentieth century, but she was certainly better off than her contemporaries in Assyria, and even than many women in some parts of the East today. She was never segregated and made to live in stultifying isolation, but shared many of the feasts and celebrations which the rest of the family enjoyed. As we shall see, she worked incredibly hard, but her place in the home was not that of the unpaid domestic servant. She was essentially the mother of the sons of the house and this status won for her privileges commensurate with its great responsibilities.

MARRIAGE

It comes as something of a surprise to realize that the Old Testament not only countenances polygamy, but assumes that in fact many men (if not most) keep two wives (Deuteronomy 21. 15). There is, incidentally, no word in the Hebrew language for bachelor. In theory, an Israelite could have as many wives as he wished, but in practice only kings and the wealthy could

69

afford more than two. It seems certain, however, that the Israelite who was loyal to the religion of Moses married only one wife, in accordance with the ideal made explicit in the teaching of the prophets. They would never have described the relationship between God and Israel as a *marriage* (as Hosea does, for example), if they had recognized polygamy as the normal and legitimate practice. The poor man, in any case, never had more than one wife (whatever his religious convictions), because payment for a bride had to be made to her father or guardian. Scholars still debate whether this payment constituted an outright cash purchase, or whether it represented a gift which compensated the father for the loss of his daughter and sealed the bond of alliance between the two families. The distinction must often have been a fine one to draw. Whatever the exact significance of this payment, it could be "worked off", as when Jacob served Laban fourteen years for Rachel and Leah.

Although marriage was essentially a legal and not a religious institution, there is no direct evidence that formal written contracts were made. It is only much later that we hear of marriage licences (Tobit 7. 14). The marriage was formally arranged, however, by the bridegroom's people and not by the young man himself. The theoretical objections to this practice are obvious, but, nevertheless, it didn't prevent Jacob from falling for Rachel at first sight when they met at the well and the seven years he served her father (whatever its legal significance) "seemed unto him but a few days, for the love he had to her" (Genesis 29. 20). The Israelites, as we might have guessed, married young. Professor Köhler has calculated that on the average a man was a father at 19, a grandfather at 38 and a great-grandfather at 57!

From the moment of their formal betrothal, the young couple were married and not simply engaged. There was, however, sometimes an interval before they began to live together and it was during this period that the man was exempt from military service (see p. 146). The actual wedding ceremony consisted of the bridegroom's bringing the bride to his own home. Specially dressed for the occasion, he set off in procession with his friends to meet the bride at her father's house. The bride, veiled and in a wedding-dress, was accompanied by bridesmaids and sometimes by her personal maids, when she came of a wealthy

22   The one-roomed Cottage of a Peasant

family and these were part of the dowry she received from her
father. Her jewellery would be the bridegroom's present, which
custom appears to have demanded. The wedding procession
returned to the bridegroom's house (with what hilarity and
singing we are left to imagine) and then there began a gargantuan
feast which lasted anything up to a week, or even a fortnight
(Judges 14. 12). We are not told how the wedding guests spent
all this time, but the flavour of their celebrations may be
gathered from Psalm 45, which was written as an anthem for
a royal wedding, and from the lyrics of the Song of Songs.
We must bear in mind, however, that both these pieces are for
elaborate weddings at a later period.

HOUSES

In what kind of house did the young couple make their
home?

When one examines the house-plans of the Israelite cities
which have been excavated, the overwhelming impression is
that most people lived in a terribly overcrowded and impoverished condition. A large family often lived, worked, had
their meals and slept in a single room, which was also shared
for some part of the year by one or two sheep and goats(22).
In the dark winter months, it was ill-lit and suffocating (for
there were no chimneys for the fire); in the summer, it was

infested with insects. Only when we have associated in our minds the average Israelite dwelling with (say) a crofter's cottage in Scotland or an Irish peasant's cabin, as they existed within living memory, is it safe to take into account the detailed information which can be gleaned from the Old Testament. Inevitably, much of this reflects the conditions of kings and noblemen, as do the remains of the well-built palaces and residences unearthed on the ancient sites.

The poorer people in Old Testament times certainly lived in a one-roomed cottage, of which the congestion was relieved only by a small yard in front, where most of the daily domestic work was done(32). Although their sheep and goats were also intended to spend most of their time in the yard, they strayed into the house and were brought in for shelter during bad weather. Not that the house itself provided complete protection from the elements. Being built largely of mud, it leaked whenever it rained hard; hence the proverb which likens the difficulty of keeping the water out with the difficulty of controlling a nagging wife:

A continual dropping in a very rainy day
And a contentious woman are alike (Proverbs 27. 15).

The roof, which was made of brushwood overlaid with earth and clay, had to be rolled after every downpour. For this purpose, a cylindrical roller (like a small garden-roller) was always kept ready, as it is still in Syria. How flimsy these flat roofs were may be judged by the story of the palsied man at Capernaum, for whom the roof was quickly broken up (Mark 2. 4). Mud was also the material used for the floor, which was stamped hard and sometimes consolidated with limestone chips.

On the analogy of Eastern houses today, the Israelite peasant's house is usually represented as containing a raised platform on which the women of the family did their work. It is by no means certain that this was the usual arrangement in this period, although something of the kind may be suggested by the fact that the roof was often 9 to 12 feet above the level of the floor. If houses had such platforms, they cannot have been very high, nor provided much protection against agile sheep and goats. Nathan seems to have been quite content to share his bowl with his ewe-lamb (II Samuel 12. 3) and there is no hint that the witch of Endor objected to having a fatted calf in her house (I Samuel 28. 24).

23 A typical Saucer Lamp

Inside, the dreary colour of the mud walls was unrelieved by sunlight. In fact, the summer sun was regarded as a bigger menace than the winter rain and so (quite contrary to our own custom), whenever possible, houses were built to face north. For the same reason, windows were few and small. As there was no glass with which to glaze them, and as they had to serve as vents for the smoke of the fire, they consisted simply of slits, perhaps with some kind of lattice or wooden shutters. The only form of lighting was the small oil lamp, of which hundreds of specimens have been excavated. It was usually no more than a saucer with a lip, pinched between the potter's thumb and forefinger, on which the wick rested (23). The wick was made of hemp or flax and the lamp oil came sometimes from animals, but more often from olives. In any case, it must have given a very dim light and been extremely unpractical. It was always kept burning, most obviously so that some form of lighter should always be to hand, because (matches not having been invented) the only way of making a light was the fire-drill and this was too awkward to be used constantly. A burning lamp was also valuable for keeping away evil spirits and this was the really weighty consideration!

The climate did not give the fire-place the central importance it enjoys with us and only the larger houses had them. We hear of a king sitting in front of his brazier in the winter (Jeremiah 36. 22), but the Hebrew language significantly makes no distinction between a fire-place and an ash-pit. In most Israelite homes, the "fire-place" was no more than a hole, dug in the mud floor, in which wood, thorns and dung-cakes were burnt.

As occupants of bed-sitting rooms have learnt in recent years, there are distinct disadvantages in sleeping in the room where you also spend the day-time. Although the big houses had separate bedrooms, ordinary people slept together in their single room. Going to bed in a large family must have been a delicate operation (like negotiating stepping-stones in a crowd) and the stuffiness, snoring and yells of teething babies must have made the nights seem long. For the most part, people

73

slept on a rug or a straw mat on the bare earthern floor, covered by the cloak they had worn in the day (Exodus 22. 27). Mattresses and bedclothes were the luxuries of kings and even royal beds were probably little more than divans or sofas raised at one end. The divan bed and the low wide chair illustrated (24, 27) are pottery models found in a tomb at Lachish. Although there is no indication of the material of which the originals were made, they give us authentic evidence of the shape of furniture in use about 700 B.C.

There was neither room to house nor money to buy much furniture. Meals were taken squatting on the ground and the "table" was usually only a mat or skin on which the food was placed. Tables and chairs were known, but, like the luxurious couches condemned by Amos (6. 4), they were beyond the pocket of the average householder. When the woman of Shunem arranged for Elisha "a bed, and a table, and a stool, and a candlestick" (II Kings 4. 10), she was pampering an honoured guest. The average one-roomed house was congested enough with its kitchen utensils, storage jars, tools and animal fodder.

From the crowded chaos of the house, the flat roof provided a much-needed escape. Here you could take the air and sometimes enjoy enough seclusion for saying your prayers. But such peace must have been rare, for the roof was a great social centre. In the congested streets of the cities, where house jostled house (21), you could easily join your neighbours on their roof or shout the gossip of the day across the narrow gap. To proclaim something upon the house-top (Matthew 10. 27) was to make a public announcement. So much was it a place of assembly that in the time of Jeremiah, altars were set up on the roof for pagan worship (Jeremiah 19. 13). Even here, you could not entirely escape evidence of the day's work. We hear of flax being dried on the roof and no doubt it was used for spreading out the washing to dry. The unexpected law in Deuteronomy is, perhaps, not so surprising after all: "When thou buildest a new house, then thou shalt make a battlement for thy roof, that thou bring not blood upon thine house, if any man fall from thence" (22. 8).

Just as we might put up a tent in the garden for sleeping out in summer, the Israelite sometimes erected an arbour of boughs on the roof of his house, thus making a temporary second story. How far permanent second stories were common, it is

24   Model Couch (from a Lachish tomb)

25   Oil flask, with cup-mouth used for dipping bread

26   Seven-wicked lamp from Ezion-geber

27   Model Chair (from a Lachish tomb)

28 Gaming-board from the Royal Graves at Ur of the Chaldees. Squares of shell are inlaid with lapis-lazuli and red limestone and set in bitumen upon wood

very difficult to decide. Some scholars think that in the second half of this period, upper stories were usual and that the head of the household slept upstairs with his family. Bigger houses certainly had upper floors. We hear, for example, of Elisha's upstairs guest room and a summer parlour (in Hebrew revealingly called the "upper chamber of cooling") is mentioned in Judges 3. 20. Also, it is reported laconically that the unfortunate Ahaziah "fell down through the lattice in his upper chamber that was in Samaria, and was sick" (II Kings 1. 2) and so, evidently, kings went upstairs to bed. In palaces and large houses, you reached the second floor by a stone staircase leading out of the courtyard; the peasant, however, probably used a wooden ladder, which he pulled up after him, as a way of locking up for the night. It has even been conjectured that some of the bigger houses had three floors, but structural problems must have made such high buildings very exceptional and very unsafe.

The wealthier citizen spent his money on building over a larger space rather than on building higher, and we have a considerable amount of information about the kind of ground plan he favoured. Usually, his house was built along the three sides of an open court, like the one in the drawing(21). In this example, we may suppose that the rooms on the left and right of the entrance were used for storing grain, wine and oil and that the living quarters were those at the back of the court. Although it is impossible to be sure of the details, the illustration gives a trustworthy general impression of a nobleman's residence in the ninth and eighth centuries B.C.

CHILDREN

The desire of every newly-married couple was children:

> As arrows in the hand of a mighty man,
> So are the children of one's youth.
> Happy is that man that hath his quiver full of them
> (Psalm 127. 4f.).

The psalmist's words apply especially to sons, who could help their father with his work and perpetuate his name and property. So important was the maintenance of the family, that if a man died childless, it was the duty of his nearest kinsman to marry his widow and raise a family "that his name

77

be not blotted out of Israel". The most explicit reference to this so-called "levirate marriage" is to be found in Deuteronomy 25. 5–10. Although it was only sons who could inherit the family estate and care for their parents in old age, daughters were by no means despised in Israel.

It is impossible to generalize about the size of the family. Seven children appears to have been the maximum for a mother, but a man who could boast more than one wife would obviously have more offspring in his quiver.

The birth of a child interrupted the mother's household work to the smallest possible extent, although we hear of midwives who attended her. The new-born baby was washed, rubbed with salt and wrapped in swaddling bands. Usually, the mother breast-fed her children, but sometimes a wet-nurse had to be called in. Nannies like Deborah, who brought up Rebekah, were to be found in wealthier households and it is pleasing to notice how securely they won a place in the family circle. The child was weaned (from our point of view) very late—when he was two or three years old, and the day of weaning was sufficiently important to provide an excuse for a family party. We have an echo of baby-talk in the Hebrew for "beloved" and "mother" and a metaphor in Isaiah tells us that children were "borne upon the side" (that is, across the hip) and "dandled upon the knees" (66. 12); otherwise, the door of the Israelite nursery is closed to us.

The name which was given to the child soon after his birth did not simply follow a current fashion, such as the indefatigable correspondent to *The Times* records annually for its readers. It was chosen with care, because it was thought to be intimately related, not only to the child's personality, but even to his fortune in life. The many personal names compounded with one of the names for God were intended as a kind of protective prayer. The change of Benjamin's name ("the son of the right hand") from Ben-oni ("the son of my sorrow"), given to him by his dying mother, was calculated to bring its owner good fortune (Genesis 35. 18). The most outstanding symbolic names are those given by the prophets to their children. To be called Maher-shalal-hash-baz ("the spoil speedeth, the prey hasteth") or Lo-ruhamah ("that hath not obtained mercy") would be difficult for any boy or girl to live down. Easier for their owners (but not much more so) were names like Dog (Caleb),

Ewe (Rachel), Bee (Deborah), Wild Cow (Leah), Mouse (Achbor) and Fish (Nun). Other names hit off physical peculiarities, like Scabby (Gareb) and Hairy (Esau). All Israelite names were personal (that is, what we call first or "Christian") names; no surnames were used, not because the family connexion was unimportant, but because it was so important as not to need mentioning.

For the first few years of their life, both boys and girls were brought up by their mothers, but boys were soon transferred to their father's discipline. The Old Testament in no way soft-pedals its rigours. It is difficult to believe that many fathers ever allowed themselves to be so outwitted by defiant sons as to be forced to invoke the capital punishment laid down in the law (Deuteronomy 21. 18–21), but a writer of the second century B.C. leaves us in no doubt that the Hebrew outlook was emphatically "Spare the rod and spoil the child":

> Pamper thy child, and he shall make thee afraid; play with him, and he will grieve thee. Laugh not with him, lest thou have sorrow with him; and thou shalt gnash thy teeth in the end. Give him no liberty in his youth . . . and beat him on the sides while he is a child, lest he wax stubborn, and be disobedient unto thee (Ecclesiasticus 30. 9–12).

We must read this advice, however, with a pinch of salt, especially in view of the fact that its author was a sententious great-grandfather, who lived at a time when it was only too easy for young men to go to the dogs. On the other side of the picture, it is fair to guess that the youngest, as well as the eldest, son received preferential treatment. In an age when there were few only sons to spoil, the son born to old parents was probably able to get a good deal of his own way.

Education, in our sense of the word, hardly existed in ancient Israel (see pp. 178 ff.), but from an early age a boy was taught to share his father's work. There were scores of jobs he could do in the fields and the vineyards and, of course, the shepherd boy was a very familiar figure. We may take it that a boy in Israel had a short childhood and as a youth was never given much leisure for sowing his wild oats. What he was denied in formal education and recreation, however, he gained in practical experience and, by having family responsibilities at an age when many boys nowadays have just left school, he matured early.

A Hebrew prophet once dreamt of an idyllic age of peace when "there shall yet old men and old women sit in the streets of Jerusalem . . . and the streets of the city shall be full of boys and girls playing" (Zechariah 8. 4f.). Unfortunately, we cannot discover what those games might have been. Excavations, however, have unearthed a number of whistles, rattles, miniature cooking utensils and pottery models of furniture and animals (24, 27, 99, 118). Children always having been what they are, these cannot all have been used exclusively for burying in tombs. Surely some were claimed as toys!

DOMESTIC ROUTINE

For Israelite society, to say that a woman's place was in the home would be less the utterance of an old-fashioned platitude than a statement of the obvious. The Book of Proverbs contains a remarkable panegyric of the loyal housewife which splendidly summarizes her bustling activity:

> She seeketh wool and flax,
> And worketh it up as she pleaseth.
> She is like the merchant-ships;
> She bringeth her food from afar.
> She riseth also while it is yet night,
> And giveth food to her household . . .
> She examineth a field, and buyeth it;
> With her earnings she planteth a vineyard . . .
> Her lamp goeth not out by night.
> She putteth out her hand to the distaff
> And layeth hold on the spindle. . . .
> She looketh well to the ways of her household,
> And eateth not the bread of idleness (31. 13–27).

This particular housewife was obviously a lady of consequence. We may take it for granted, therefore, that the more humble mother, although perhaps not able to buy property out of her earnings, was even further from eating the bread of idleness. Her two chief concerns were food and clothing for the family. Since both (as we shall see in a moment) were entirely home-made, it is not surprising that she started the day's work before dawn. No doubt, her children collected the fuel for the fire, filled and trimmed the lamps, helped (as soon as they were big enough) with the spinning, the water-carrying, and the baking. One thing at which they didn't get much practice was washing-up after

29   Women grinding Corn

meals, although one curious Old Testament metaphor represents God as threatening Jerusalem in terms which for us are reminiscent of the kitchen sink: "I will wipe Jerusalem as a man wipes a bowl, wiping it and turning it upside down" (II Kings 21. 13).

There was, however, other washing to be done, although the Old Testament could not be called expansive on the subject of laundry. Its only direct reference reveals the fact that during Saul's absence, his son had *not* washed his clothes (II Samuel 19. 24)! As still happens in backward parts of Europe, presumably the women took their bundles of washing to a spring outside the city—the primitive equivalent of the communal "launderette". A soap of sorts was known (see p. 125), but the housewife's methods at the spring were probably more abrasive than detergent.

FOOD AND DRINK

A list of the various foods eaten in this period would no more give a true impression of everyday meals than would the catalogue of an expensive London grocer today. Most people had to live on what they could scratch out of the unwilling soil and famine was always round the corner. Bread and food are interchangeable terms in the Old Testament and coarse barley "loaves" were undoubtedly the staple diet of the peasant. Wheat bread was preferred, but it was, of course, more expensive.

30 Saddle Quern and Muller for grinding grain

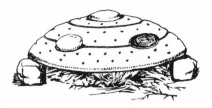

31   The simplest form of Oven

Every day was baking day in a Hebrew household and bread-making must have taken up a great deal of the time and energy of the women folk. They first had to grind the ears into meal. This was a back-aching business before the invention of the heavy rotary mill. It is possible that even the simple mill with the upper and lower stones(29) only came into general use in the fourth century B.C. and that the usual apparatus in our period was either the pestle and mortar or the saddle quern and muller(30), which the women used in a kneeling position. The coarse meal thus produced was mixed with salt and water and made into dough. Unleavened cakes were the quickest and easiest to make, but generally the mixture was leavened with some of the fermented dough kept from the previous day's baking. It was then left to rise.

The methods of baking varied. In the open country, the dough was made into "ash cakes" on stones heated by a wood-and-dung fire and covered over with ashes; such was Elijah's un-appetizing diet in the desert (I Kings 19. 6). Normally, however, some form of oven was used. The simplest consisted of a large earthenware convex plate or shallow bowl placed upside down over a fire and resting on a number of stones. A specimen found at Mizpah was *almost* pierced with innumerable small holes to conduct the heat better. The dough was made into thin pancakes, which were baked on the top of the plate(31). The second type of oven and the one most used was essentially a large earthenware jar, often plastered with mud and potsherds on the outside, *inside* which a fire was made(32). It was either sunk in the ground or (as in the drawing) placed on a mud surface; in either case, the only air vent was the hole at the top. When the fire had died down, the women popped their thin sheets of dough on to the hot inner surface of the oven, where they stuck until they were sufficiently baked.

These thin sheets of bread must have been difficult to pack to take to work or on a journey. It is not surprising, therefore, that "parched corn"; that is, fresh ears lightly roasted, should have been so popular. It was the ancient equivalent of

82

sandwiches. For special occasions, the baking included cakes and pastry. Sometimes the dough was mixed with olive oil or cooked in it and sometimes wafers were made with honey (sugar, of course, was unknown). The "cracknels" given by the queen to the prophet (I Kings 14. 3) may possibly have been cakes sprinkled with aromatic seeds. Recently excavated juglets with perforated bottoms could certainly have been used as sprinklers for such fancy baking.

The next most important of the woman's daily chores was the supply of drinking water. A fortunate household might possess its own cistern hewn out of the solid rock—that was everybody's dream (II Kings 18. 31), like refrigerators nowadays. The rain water which collected in such cisterns must often have been worse than the drinking water of the old sailing ships, but not a drop of water could be despised. Otherwise, the supply had to be carried from a spring or well. Hebrew engineers showed great skill and ingenuity in mining tunnels to give access to water springs in time of siege (see pp. 137 ff.), but during our period they never succeeded in devising any machine for raising the water. It was still drawn from wells by hand

32 Baking Bread. One woman grinds the wheat, while another stirs, the dough. A tray of flat loaves is being carried away, as the children refuel the fire inside the oven

33 Women at the Well

in a leather bucket suspended on a length of rope. As cities were built on mounds, the women had to trudge down to (and up from!) the spring outside the walls, or else negotiate the steps leading down to the well inside the city. It was hard work with a water pot on your head or shoulder and the drudgery was lightened only by the opportunity it provided for meeting your friends (33).

Since water was scarce and not very palatable, a good deal of milk was drunk. It came from goats and sheep. Hebrew has a word for fresh milk, but in the climate of Palestine it cannot have been used as much as another term meaning sour

84

milk or curds. As soon as the fresh milk was put into the goat-skin bottle, it thickened slightly and went sour. All the better, it was thought, for quenching the thirst. The word for curds also means butter, which was made by rocking the skin of milk to and fro (Proverbs 30. 33). Butter, of course, would not keep in the heat of Palestine and so it was clarified and stored as a liquid in skins. The Hebrew housewife also made cheese. We do not hear much about it in this period, but when we are told that David took ten "cuts of milk" to his brothers at the front (I Samuel 17. 18), it is probable that fresh-milk cheeses are meant.

Next, after bread and milk, in the ordinary Israelite's diet came vegetables. Despite our curious lack of direct information, there must have been a considerable variety. The Hebrews almost certainly cultivated "the cucumbers, and the melons, and the leeks, and the onions, and the garlic", which they represented their forefathers as pining for in the wilderness after they had left Egypt (Numbers 11. 5). Evidently, the popular palate went in for strong flavours, as we may also conclude from the use of spices—like coriander and black cummin, which took the place of pepper. Without them, the familiar stews of lentils and beans would have become intolerably boring.

Stewing, rather than roasting, was the usual method of cooking, even on the very rare festive occasions when the average Israelite ate meat. The kitchens of the Temple described by Ezekiel are literally "boiling-houses" and the familiarity of the deep round bowl in excavated cities confirms the evidence that in Palestine to cook almost invariably meant to boil. The same method is reflected in the curious law which lays it down that a kid should not be boiled in its mother's milk (Exodus 23. 19), a prohibition, incidentally, arising from the fact that this was part of a forbidden Canaanite religious rite. The law imposed further limitations on the eating of meat. Animals were classified as clean and unclean (Deuteronomy 14. 3ff.) and certain birds were also excluded (14. 11ff.). Even clean animals could not be eaten if they had died a natural death or had been killed by a wild beast; and at all times great care had to be taken to drain the carcase of its sacred blood. Whenever the ordinary Israelite had meat for dinner, it was eaten as part of a religious sacrificial feast and the victim was most commonly

34 Waiters carrying Pomegranates and Locusts on Skewers

a sheep or a goat. Beef from specially fattened animals was reserved (like the fatted calf of the Prodigal Son) for great feasts given by the wealthy. Even the wealthy were denied the pleasure of a feather-light omelette, since hens and their eggs were as yet unknown.

For dessert, the Hebrews enjoyed a plentiful and varied supply of fruit. Grapes were eaten *au naturel* as well as in the form of raisins; the first ripe fig was a great delicacy and cakes of dried figs were included in the soldier's rations. It is fairly safe to guess that dates were familiar in earlier as in later times and there is no doubt that pomegranates were relished for their refreshing juice. The drawing (34) shows how they were arranged for Assyrian feasts. The first waiter is carrying locusts threaded on a skewer, as frogs are in French cooking. How the Hebrews served locusts we do not know, but they were certainly eaten.

The housewife had the whole of the day in which to prepare and cook the family's food, since the main meal was taken in the evening, about sunset, after the "burden and heat of the day". The only other proper meal was eaten at noon. There is no reference in the Old Testament to any earlier breakfast, although it is hard to believe that the morning's work was done on a completely empty stomach.

The drinking of wine was universal. Taking it with water or luxuriously iced with snow from the mountains were later customs and even then the latter can hardly have been a part of *everyday* life. The ordinary Israelite in our period took his wine in its natural state or (like the Assyrians) mingled with spices and drugs to increase its "headiness". It is not surprising that the Old Testament contains so many warnings about drinking

86

to excess. The men of Israel also drank pomegranate wine and (possibly) wine made from dates. They do not appear, however, to have been great beer-drinkers. In this respect, they differed from their neighbours, the Philistines, whose beer-mugs with strainer spouts have been found by the hundred.

DRESS

Home dress-making, nowadays, is an affair of sewing machines, paper patterns and materials bought by the yard. In Old Testament times, it began with the flax in the field and the wool on the sheep's back. After cleaning, carding, spinning and weaving (see pp. 116–21), the Israelites understandably set a high value on clothes. A "goodly Babylonish mantle" tempted Achan no less than silver and gold (Joshua 7. 21) and Samson offered a prize of "thirty linen garments and thirty changes of raiment" to the winner of his riddle contest (Judges 14. 12). Then, as now, dress enabled the *nouveaux riches* to display their affluence and Isaiah was not the only prophet to speak out against the vulgar extravagance of women, "with stretched forth necks and wanton eyes, walking and mincing as they go, and making a tinkling with their feet" (3. 16). Even men are accused of adopting the latest foreign fashions.

One need only consider the ambiguity in English of such familiar terms as coat, tunic, overalls and vest to appreciate that the exact details of Hebrew clothes are likely to escape us. The many Hebrew terms describing articles of dress almost certainly overlapped and changed their meaning. Only an illustrated and annotated fashion journal from Old Jerusalem could decide the many disputed points which arise and the best we possess is a small number of pictorial monuments (mostly from Egypt and Assyria), which depict Asiatics and Israelites in various humiliating situations. Inevitably, these representations are stylized, somewhat in the manner of a cartoon, and may be relied on only for their general lines.

The main out-door garment for both men

35 The "Shawl" as worn by the Israelite woman in the eighth century B.C.

87

and women was a shapeless cloak, not unlike a Roman toga. For the most part, it would be made of heavy woollen cloth, but it is very likely that the version worn by peasants and shepherds in rough weather was made of goat or sheep skins. The ordinary cloak, however, seems to have been sufficiently substantial to serve as a rug for sitting on and for sleeping in at night. The cloaks of the Israelites accompanying Jehu on the ninth-century Black Obelisk(3) are less voluminous and look much more like a fringed shawl. The women's cloaks were even more obviously of the shawl variety, draped from head to foot, as the Assyrian reliefs illustrate(35, 84). From the law forbidding men and women to exchange dress (Deuteronomy 22. 5), we know that their clothes were not identical, but all the evidence suggests that they were very much alike in their general design. Women's cloaks were probably longer and more highly decorated than those of their husbands.

36 A Canaanite lady of about 1200 B.C. Notice her hair style and long tunic

The main (and probably the only) garment worn under the cloak was a close-fitting tunic made of wool or linen. It had sleeves, which in the case of Joseph's famous tunic (the traditional "coat of many colours") were long; we may compare it with that of the Canaanite lady depicted on an ivory from Megiddo(36). The tunic came down to the knees (or even lower) and was fastened at the waist by a girdle of leather or cloth. Either in the folds above the tunic belt or in the folds of the outer cloak (and probably in both), the Israelite kept his money and knick-knacks—the precious objects which the modern man keeps in his pockets and his wife in her handbag. The psalmist refers to this "pocket", when he says, "render unto our neighbours sevenfold into their bosom" (79. 12); in other words, "pay them back". Another familiar Biblical expression—"gird up thy loins" (II Kings 4. 29) is connected with the tunic and originates in the practice of tucking it up into the belt for active movement. Workers not only girded their loins, but, as now, discarded their cloaks and got down to it in their shirt sleeves. In the Beni-Hasan painting(11), the tunics of both men and women are ornate and brightly coloured, whereas those depicted in the Lachish reliefs are severely plain(35). It is probable that this contrast represents a change of style and not simply the personal impressions of two different artists.

It is unlikely that the Israelites habitually wore any under-clothes in our sense of the word, although the tunic was re-garded by them as an undergarment; to appear in it alone was to appear improperly dressed. The "waist cloth", which seems to be a development of the simple loin-cloth, was a forerunner of the tunic and not an additional undergarment. In the Beni-Hasan picture(11), it looks rather like a skirt or (*pace* the Scots!) a kilt; a man in the Lachish relief(37) is similarly clad. Possibly the latter figure was intended to represent an Israelite warrior and the "kilt" survived the introduction of the long tunic as a part of military dress.

The fact that the Assyrian reliefs almost invariably depict Israelites as humiliated captives, and, therefore, as bare-foot has deprived us of information about Hebrew foot-wear. The sandals of the men in the Beni-Hasan painting give us a fair impression of the Israelite's sandals, but very few women in our period would have been able to afford the comfortable-looking boots depicted there. Seal-skin shoes were the last word in fashion (Ezekiel 16. 10). The general position may be judged by the fact that a pair of shoes was a proverbial expression for something of small value (like our "tuppence" or "two pins"); to go barefoot was a mark of abject poverty.

37 An Israelite captive wearing a "kilt" and turban

Considering the cruel blaze of the Palestinian sun, one would naturally expect more explicit evidence about headgear than is forthcoming. The figures of the Beni-Hasan painting are bareheaded and the care devoted to hair dressing suggests that hats were by no means always worn. The Israelites depicted on the Black Obelisk(3), however, wear what have been described as "stocking caps", while a century and a half later, the men of Lachish wear a kind of turban. It is tempting to guess (though guess it is) that some equivalent of the modern Bedouin *keffiyeh* was also used, that is, a square of linen or wool, folded triangularly and fixed round the head with a cord. It protects not only the head, but the cheeks and neck.

Cloak, tunic, girdle, sandals and headdress complete the average Israelite's wardrobe. It will be noticed that nothing corresponding to a nightshirt or nightdress is included, since the Hebrew family stripped before going to sleep and wrapped themselves in their outdoor cloaks. The more penetrating student of feminine attire will find much to whet his curiosity in the catalogue of Isaiah 3. 18–23. It should, however, be borne in mind that this formidable collection is intended as a deliberate caricature and certainly has no bearing on everyday conditions. Nevertheless, some of the jewellery listed by the satirical commentator has been discovered in recent excavations and there is no doubt that the average Israelite woman could and did acquire a whole range of fairly cheap personal ornaments—beads of semi-precious stones, bone pendants, bracelets, anklets and rings (in both bronze and iron) to be worn on her ears, her fingers and her nose. Some of her combs have also been unearthed.

It is not easy to fathom Hebrew hair styles. The men allowed their hair to grow long and thick, like the fine-looking Canaanite captives on the Egyptian relief from the temple of Rameses III (115). They also set great store by their beards, which were regarded as a mark of manly dignity. This does not mean, however, that barbers could be dispensed with. Although they are only mentioned once in the Old Testament, the tools of their trade—razors for shaving—are often referred to. In Ezekiel, priests are instructed to have their hair cut neither too long nor too short and so presumably there were experts who knew how to keep their customers within the letter of the law. As shaving off the beard was a sign of mourning, and as razors must have been costly, it is fairly safe to assume that there was work enough for one or two barbers in every Israelite city. Only such unreliable witnesses as pottery figurines record the hair style adopted by Israelite women. The photograph of the Mother Goddess(117) suggests three or more rows of rather stiff curls across the forehead and fairly short locks at the sides; on the other hand, the lady from Megiddo(36) wore her hair long.

TOILET

It is probable that there was a good deal of overlapping between the hairdressing trade and that of the perfumer, as indeed there is with us. The twentieth century can teach the ancient East nothing about the use of hair-oils. Ointments,

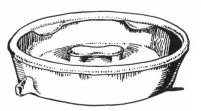

38　A Foot-bath from Samaria with a centre support

salves, oils and creams of every description must have been almost as familiar and as necessary a part of everyday life in this period as bread. Workers needed them as sunburn lotions and as a protection against flies and vermin; they learnt, it would seem, to tolerate lice, but fleas they hated. And for those who had the money to spend, the sweet spices and aromatic gums imported from Arabia were a desirable defence against less gratifying smells.

The notorious Jezebel who "painted her eyes" (II Kings 9. 30) was not the only woman in Old Testament times to use make-up (compare Jeremiah 4. 30). Palettes for mixing cosmetics (such as the black antimony and olive oil probably used by Jezebel) are among the more frivolous finds of the Palestinian archaeologists. So far, however, they have not found a sufficient number of polished bronze hand-mirrors to suggest that every woman who painted her face was able to sit and admire it.

The hot climate and dusty roads of Palestine must have demanded frequent washing, but we are ill-informed about the details. It seems that official guest-houses were sometimes equipped with built-in wash basins (see p. 64) and portable foot-baths were known (38). What happened in ordinary families, we can only guess, but probably more oil than water was used.

RECREATIONS

The sports enthusiast will find little to engage his interest in the daily life of Israel. The Old Testament knows nothing of ball games, and the athletic contests and gymnasia of the Greeks shocked the conservative Jews when they were introduced to Palestine in the third and second centuries B.C. It is possible, however, that young men had wrestling-matches (as they did in

Egypt) and, perhaps, as Professor Kennett proposed, "the story of Jacob's wrestling and the device resorted to by his opponent when the latter found himself unable to gain the mastery, suggests definite wrestling rules, and that it was not 'playing the game' to grip 'below the belt'" (Genesis 32. 24–26). It is also more than probable that the Israelites' tall, spare, physique made them good at sprinting. Such evidence of sportsmanship is, however, extremely meagre and it is questionable whether it can be augmented by hunting and fishing, since the Hebrews engaged in these activities less for amusement than from necessity (see pp. 112–15).

Recreation was found, rather, in what we should naturally think of as indoor amusements—feasting, music and dancing, although these were mainly enjoyed in the open air. The Israelite, it seems, did not take his pleasures as seriously as we do. His gambling instincts found their outlet in means less grave (and costly) than either Association Football or horse racing; he appears to have been satisfied with a few simple dice and gaming-boards. At Mizpah, a "little system of squares" was found scratched into the smooth rock and it is conjectured that pebbles were used for the game instead of draughts or chessmen. Such pieces and a dice have been found, however, in the ruins of another city(39). A more ambitious gaming-board has been unearthed at Megiddo. It is made of ivory in the shape of a violin and pierced with holes clearly intended for some kind of peg(40). We are as much in the dark about the rules of this game as we are about that played on the magnificently inlaid board found at Ur of the Chaldees(28). The latter dates from before 3000 B.C., but in these matters fashions do not change much.

The Israelite cast away his daily cares most characteristically, however, in giving and receiving hospitality. Every possible excuse was taken for throwing a party—the arrival of a guest, the weaning of a child and probably (though not certainly) family birthdays. There were, of course, in addition, the annual religious festivals, which, for a people who made little distinction between everyday life and religious life, were always great social occasions (see pp. 228–30). The order and

39   Dice and Gaming Pieces

92

ceremonies of a feast must have been less formal in this period than they became later (see, for example, Ecclesiasticus 31. 12–18 and 32. 1–13), but we may be confident that as each guest arrived his feet were washed and his head anointed with oil. Arrangements for the meal itself varied

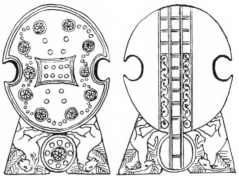

40, 41   The front and back of an Ivory Gaming-Board from Megiddo

according to circumstances. During Old Testament times, all the great feasts were supposed to be held at the local sanctuary, for all meat-eating was sacrificial in character. It is difficult to estimate how far this principle was disregarded, but it is evident that those who could best afford to eat meat would be the least likely to worry about its religious significance. At an open-air feast, the guests would sit on the ground round the mat which did duty as a table and the meal would be taken picnic fashion. At more sophisticated banquets held indoors, the food would be served at very low tables and the guests would sit on chairs, or even (in degenerate society) recline on couches. The order of precedence among the guests was worked out with great deliberation and the chief persons of the feast were given the choicest (and largest!) portions of the food. At ordinary family parties, men and women feasted together, but it would seem that the ladies were excluded from more formal gatherings.

With the wine-drinking (which is the literal meaning of the Hebrew for feasting), went music and dancing. We are not to think, however, of anything in the nature of a modern dinner-dance, since the men and women danced separately in what must often have been an odd combination of exuberance, cabaret performance and religious ritual.

Israelite feasts ended, no doubt, as noisily as regimental or boat-club dinners and the older members of the party would retire to quiet corners to talk. The Hebrews were great raconteurs and their frequent comments on the wagging tongue show that they were not unaware of its dangers. It is only after our period that we have direct evidence for "contests of wits" over the wine after dinner, but the pungent proverbs and riddles of the Jews have a history going back to and beyond the beginning of Old Testament times. Taste in humour is very much a national phenomenon (as the gulf between *Punch* and *The New Yorker* clearly suggests), but few can read (say)

> As the going up a sandy way is to the feet of the aged,
> So is a wife full of words to a quiet man

and conclude that the Israelite was entirely a dull dog.

MOURNING

Death was a more familiar part of daily life in Israel than it is with us, for the simple reason that families were larger and lived together under one roof. Infant mortality appears to have been exceptionally heavy and excavations have revealed the skeletons of many children buried in earthenware jars. Despite the remarkable claims for the longevity of the Patriarchs, few people lived to a ripe old age. The psalmist thought "three score years and ten" the average limit of a man's life and pitied the labour and sorrow of the octogenarian. It is probable that war, malnutrition and disease accounted for many much earlier deaths.

A death in a household set in motion a remarkably elaborate and stylized ceremony of mourning which lasted a week or more. The members of the family and their friends gathered round the dead person and indulged in lamentations bordering on hysteria. They tore their clothes, put on coarse hair garments ("sackcloth") and disfigured themselves with dust and ashes. They shaved off their hair and their beards and even brought blood by scratching themselves in paroxysms of grief. Such rites, however, went beyond the natural expression of grief (even allowing for the Israelites' highly emotional temperament) and clearly had their origin and probably their continued vitality in the fear of the spirits of the departed. This explains why professional mourners were called in to assist the family with their dirges.

The hot climate necessitated immediate burial. The Israelites did not practise either embalming or cremation, but they attached the highest importance to decent burial. The body, fully clothed but without a coffin, was taken by the funeral

94

party to its grave. Sometimes this was inside the city walls and sometimes in the courtyard of the house, but usually it was made in or near the city mound. The ideal was for a man to be "gathered to his fathers" in the most literal sense of being laid in a family vault, but no doubt only the wealthy could afford such a luxury. The poor were buried in common graves or in hillside caves. Inevitably, it is about the more elaborate tombs that archaeology has supplied most information. Generally, these consisted of a series of underground chambers dug out of the soft limestone rock. You entered by a low door and went down a slope or a few steps to a central room from which other smaller chambers led off. These were provided with rock benches on which the bodies were laid. The outer door was sealed by a thick stone slab fitted to the opening and kept in position by a boulder. The flat wheel-shaped type of stone door which you rolled to one side in a groove was not used for tombs until just before the period of the New Testament. Many tombs had been in use for centuries and were periodically enlarged and cleared. Old bones were then collected and put into pits dug in the floor of the tomb.

The mourners left with the body a variety of everyday objects—weapons, lamps, jewellery and kitchen equipment such as jars, jugs and dishes. It is from tombs that models of Israelite furniture have been recovered(24, 27). The purpose underlying these deposits is very difficult to determine. Originally, it is likely that they were intended to equip the dead person for his life beyond the grave, but during our period archaeologists report that the articles became less and less realistic and, significantly enough, there appears to be no evidence that the jars and jugs ever contained food or drink. It seems that the crude notion of fitting out the dead with material for their new life had been abandoned and that the deposits were no more than a symbolic survival of old custom. Even today, it is not unknown for a headmaster to be buried with his academic dress on the top of his coffin. The value of the tomb deposits, especially when they included jewellery, was a fatal temptation to the unscrupulous and even the care taken to seal or hide the door of the tomb was not proof against the professional grave robber.

During the period of mourning, fasting was broken only by the funeral feast (see Jeremiah 16. 7). This was probably held at the tomb itself on the day of burial and, again, may have been the survival of a custom formerly charged with religious significance. In orthodox circles which had abandoned the practice of making offerings to the dead, the only other possible act of filial piety was the erection of a monument. That such memorials were not unknown, at least among the families of the nobility, is established by a note in II Samuel 18. 18:

> Now Absalom in his life time had taken and reared up for himself the pillar, which is in the king's dale: for he said, I have no son to keep my name in remembrance: and he called the pillar after his own name: and it is called Absalom's monument, unto this day.

The average Israelite, however, had sons and was too poor for monuments. His only memorial and hope for the future were in his family and People. Once he had brought his years to an end as a tale that is told, he entered Sheol, where his mere existence was a denial of life. But his family and People lived on and he in them, until the day when his children's children would inherit the everlasting joy and felicity of the Kingdom of God.

Chapter V

COUNTRY LIFE

THERE did not yet exist in Old Testament times the great gulf between the townsman and the countryman with which we are familiar and which was strikingly demonstrated in England by war-time evacuation. Many children from the great cities then met sheep and cows for the first time in their lives, while their lonely mothers realized with a shock how much they had grown to rely on the amenities and congestion of urban society.

The country life of the Hebrews was, in varying degrees, shared by villagers and townsmen alike, for villages were simply the suburbs of cities, and became flooded each summer by nearly the whole population. Even in winter, the men went daily *from* the town *to* the country to work in the fields, which explains why the psalmist speaks of "going out" and "coming in" in that order. The modern business man, who uses a village as a dormitory, goes home from work in the opposite direction. In ancient Israel, the vital distinction was, therefore, less that between villagers and townsmen than that between the farmer and the semi-nomad, who still wandered on the fringe of the desert and had not a home (except his tent) to call his own. It is true that the growing industries were beginning to demand a certain number of specialized workers, but there were few Israelites whose roots (so to speak) were not still in the soil.

The Hebrew year was divided, not by the Budget and Bank Holidays, but by seed-time and harvest; and it is significant that it ended after the gathering of the crops in the autumn. The pattern of religious life was also determined by the farmer's year and its three most ancient feasts were associated with the harvest of barley, wheat and summer fruits (see pp. 228–30).

It is not easy to determine the farmer's social status. In all probability, it declined during this period and the later view of the "people of the land", which set them low in the social scale, appears to have been reflected back on to the Old Testament record of earlier times. When the Israelites first occupied Palestine, they exchanged the community life of the tribe and clan for a kind of existence in which private property assumed a new importance. Grazing land was still held in common, but hard jobs like cultivating the ground and making vineyards were not worth doing unless, in the end, the property was your own. The land, therefore, was parcelled out into small farms, which were jealously handed down in families from generation to generation. The increasing prosperity of the settlers soon led, however, to the growth of a new wealthy class, which tried to buy out the small peasant proprietors and combine the old family farms into huge estates. It was to this unscrupulous section of society that the eighth-century prophet Micah was referring, when he denounced those who "covet fields, and seize them; and houses, and take them away: and they oppress a man and his house, even a man and his heritage" (2. 2). The famous story of Naboth's vineyard (I Kings 21. 1–16) shows how defenceless the peasant proprietor was in the face of wealth and power and how he fought for his rights to the bitter end. The end, indeed, was nearly always bitter, since most Israelite farmers lived on the verge of bankruptcy, so that it needed only one or two bad harvests to reduce them to slavery.

Farmers lived from hand to mouth in the most literal sense; that is to say, they grew what they needed for food. Their main crops were barley and wheat for bread, grapes for wine and raisins, and olives for their indispensable oil. This programme kept them busy for the greater part of the year. Such, at least, was the view of the village scribe who gave one of his pupils a kind of agricultural calendar to copy out as a writing exercise some time in the tenth century B.C. The boy's efforts were discovered about fifty years ago on a limestone plaque now known as the "Gezer Calendar" (60). It is not easy to decipher and certain words in it are disputed, but the following version (translated by Professor W. F. Albright) has considerable authority:

> His two months are (olive) harvest;
> his two months are planting (grain);
> his two months are late planting;
> his month is hoeing up of flax;
> his month is harvest of barley;
> his month is harvest and festivity;
> his two months are vine-tending;
> his month is summer-fruit.

42   A yoke of Oxen ploughing

Even though it is difficult to square this list with the order of the agricultural year, it does at least show that the farmer had his work cut out and that educated people in the time of Solomon were not as snobbish about work on the land as they afterwards became.

CEREALS

The preparation of the land for sowing began as soon as the "former rains" began to soften the parched earth in the autumn. The farmer then got out his plough. It was a much lighter implement than the one with which we are familiar and it consisted essentially of a wooden stake with a handle for the ploughman to hold at the top and at the bottom a metal tip (the plough-point), which from time to time had to be sharpened (see pp. 127f.). This stake was slotted through one end of a pole or shaft, at the other end of which there was fixed the yoke for the plough team. The illustration (42) shows the simplest form of yoke. The kind now used in Palestine is made of a single beam, shaped to the necks of the animals, with two pairs of wooden rods set in it at right angles so that they come down and fit on either of the animal's neck (as in illustration 44). The shaft of the plough was firmly lashed to the top of the yoke. The ploughman steered his team and kept it moving with a metal-tipped goad (64). Although a team of two oxen was

99

preferred, not every farmer could afford them and the law which forbids the yoking together of an ox and an ass (Deuteronomy 22. 10) only goes to show what often happened.

The next operation was sowing(43). The seed was not drilled in furrows, but sown broadcast and afterwards, as a precaution against ants and other pests, it was either ploughed in or raked by means of a branch or bush which was dragged over the ground. Harrowing proper does not seem to have been known in the period. The different varieties of seed, were, of course, sown at different times during the winter months and some even as late as March. Winter must have been a rather miserable time for the farming family. Breaking up stony ground and sowing in heavy rain were hard and unenviable jobs and at this season the fate of the seed and young crops often gave cause for anxiety. Violent downpours and hail storms could (literally) wash out all the farmer's labour and the uncertain climate threatened the new shoots with mildew and "blasting", the latter from the scorching Sirocco. Caterpillars were another menace.

The coming of harvest was welcomed with general relief. It began with the gathering of the barley sometime in April or May, but the exact time naturally depended on the weather and

the situation of the farm. The wheat ripened about a month after the barley. At this time, the long scythe had not been invented, but the reaper already had a better implement than the primitive wooden sickle lined with flint teeth. Thanks to the expanding use of iron for ordinary implements, his sickle, though still short and in many ways slow and inconvenient, was, nevertheless, sharp. In reaping(125), the farmer grasped the grain with his left hand and lopped off

43 Sowing broadcast

44   A Village Threshing-floor

the stalks fairly high up; he then bound them into sheaves.
The crop growing in the corners of the field, where it was
difficult to get at, and the corn which had fallen loose on the
ground were always left as a gift for the gleaners, who waited
at the edge of the field until they were given the signal to come
and gather their share.

The sheaves were taken either by asses or in carts (84) to the
threshing-floor, which was usually the common property of the
community and held that place of honour in village life which
still belongs in a few oases of industrial Britain to the village
green. More often than not, the threshing-floor was a circular
patch of ground, drained and stamped hard, on a site which
caught the prevailing west wind as it blew in from the sea.
At all times of the year it was a meeting-place (like the gate of
a city), but at threshing time, it was the centre of the whole life
of the community. (The illustration (44) shows only a single
family, so as not to mask everything else.) "Thou shalt not
muzzle the ox when he treadeth out the grain" was the ruling
of the law on the simplest method of threshing. The use of the

101

threshing sledge was common, however, and much more effective. As its name suggests, this implement was a simple hard-wood sledge curved up at the front with jagged splinters of stone or iron underneath. As it was dragged round the threshing-floor by oxen, it chopped the straw at the same time as it loosened the grain. Sometimes the driver would sit and even sleep at his work, and as you can imagine, the children found it a first-class roundabout.

When the threshing was finished, the grain was still mixed with broken straw and chaff, from which it had to be separated by winnowing. With a wooden fork or shovel, the chopped mixture was tossed into the wind, which blew the light chaff a fair distance, and the straw not quite so far, while the heavy grain fell to the ground again in a heap. Some of the straw was then put into bags and stored for use as fodder in the winter; the rest was mixed with dung and made into flat sun-dried cakes for fuel.

The grain still needed a final cleaning before it was ready for storage. This was done with simple sieves made of wooden hoops and meshes of leather thongs, which retained the refuse (such as pebbles and bits of mud) and allowed the ears to fall to the ground (45). As grain was the farmer's most valuable possession, his creditors and the tax-collector were much in evidence at this stage of the proceedings, waiting to claim their payments in kind.

If it is properly stored away from damp, grain keeps for a number of years. By an odd accident of history, the excavators of Jericho found the remains of millet, barley and lentils in round clay bins, where they had been stored 5,000 years ago! One common method of storage was in underground silos. These were often dug in the shape of a bottle several yards deep and in the excavated sites are difficult to distinguish from water cisterns. Both silos and cisterns were lined with small stones, but the latter were also carefully water-proofed with coats of lime-mortar. The narrow "necks" of these silos were covered over as a precaution against

45 Sieving grain

102

theft and sometimes, one suspects, in an attempt to evade the income tax authorities. Corn collected for the national revenue was stored at centres throughout the country in large silos or specially constructed buildings. How these were designed we are left to speculate. Long low chambers have been identified as granaries, but if Mesopotamian and Egyptian practice is anything to go by, some grain stores were high and cylindrical, with ladders leading to an opening at the top where the grain was put in and a trap-door at the bottom from which it was withdrawn as required. The details, however, must remain uncertain. Of all the methods of storage, the most popular was the big earthenware jar, which every house-holder possessed (69).

VINES

According to Old Testament tradition, the vines of Palestine were among the first things which impressed the Israelites as they entered the country. The men whom Moses sent to spy out the land came "unto the valley of Eshcol, and cut down from thence a branch with one cluster of grapes, and *they bare it upon a staff between two*" (Numbers 13. 23). The account is rather reminiscent of a fisherman's tale and such a staggering experience was unlikely to be repeated. The new settlers, nevertheless, were successful in adopting Canaanite viticulture, and produced larger crops of grapes than the visitor to the Holy Land (until perhaps recently) would have supposed possible. In Old Testament times, the hillsides must have been extensively terraced and thus protected from the heavy rains which have since washed away the scanty soil. Even in the south, the parched desert region of the Negeb still bears traces of extensive vine-growing in a previous age. The vine can flourish with astonishingly little water on stony ground, if only it is carefully tended.

The nearest we can get to an ancient Hebrew vinegrowers' manual is Isaiah's "Song of the Vineyard": "My friend had a vineyard in a very fruitful hill; and he digged it, and gathered out the stones thereof, and planted it with the choicest vine, and built a tower in the midst of it, and also hewed out a winepress therein" (5. 2). The site for a new vineyard had to be laboriously cleared of stones and scrub and each year persistent briers and thorns needed hoeing. To enable the land to be kept clean, the vines were planted in rows a few feet apart. Usually,

46 A Simple Booth

the branches were allowed to trail on the soil, but as clusters of grapes formed, they were propped up either by forked sticks or on piles of flat stones. One of the Hebrew pictures of peace, when everybody would sit "*under* his vine and under his fig tree" shows that vines were sometimes trained to climb, either on trellises or buildings.

One of the most important jobs in vine-cultivation was the annual pruning, which was carried out after blossom-time, when the grapes had formed: "For afore the harvest, when the blossom is over, and the flower becometh a ripening grape, he shall cut off the sprigs with pruning-hooks, and the spreading branches shall he take away and cut down" (Isaiah 18. 5). This was the time of the year when guards were posted in vineyards to protect the ripening crop against both man and beast. Foxes and jackals had a great liking for fresh grapes and so traps were laid and "scarecrows" of white-washed stones erected in an attempt to keep them off. The watchman, who in big vineyards was specially hired for the season, took his stand either in a simple booth (46) or on the top of a more elaborate tower. Watchtowers were round stone buildings, resembling truncated windmills, with a spiral staircase running round the outside wall. Trees growing on the flat roof afforded the man on duty protection from the sun.

The fruit ripened from July onwards according to the variety of the plant and the situation of the vineyard. It was not gathered, however, until round about September, when whole families went to camp out in the vineyards (just as London families now move into the hop fields of Kent) for the biggest party of the year. The season of grape-gathering and vintage was the Israelites' annual holiday—the ancient equivalent of our summer exodus from the towns to the sea, when even the staidest elders yielded to the general hilarity.

THE VINTAGE

The ripe clusters were cut off the plant with a kind of sickle and collected in baskets, although, it would seem, a fair proportion of the crop was devoured on the spot. The attraction of the ripe grapes was such that the casual eating of them was made the subject of a solemn law in Deuteronomy: "When thou comest into thy neighbour's vineyard, then thou mayest eat grapes thy fill at thine own pleasure; but thou shalt not put any in thy vessel" (23. 24). Rumour has it that this judicious rule, limiting "tasting" to consumption on the premises, is still imposed with good effect on workers in chocolate factories!

Those grapes which reached the baskets were taken off to the wine-press near by. Here the excitement was even greater. The centre of the scene was the group of men and women who jostled and splashed each other in the press-vat, as they trod the fruit with their bare feet (47). The treaders gave voice to a special vintage shout which is thought to have originated in some ritual cry, but whatever religious significance it retained must have been drowned by the drinking songs which rang out in endless succession. Whenever possible, the press was hewn out of the solid limestone rock, otherwise pits were dug in the earth and lined with stones and mortar. The juice ran from the press-vat

47 Treading the Grapes in the Wine-press

through a channel into another trough, which was dug deeper at a lower level. In the hot September sun, fermentation began almost immediately and continued for about six weeks. In smaller vineyards, the fermenting liquid was allowed to stand for this period in the wine-vat, but where the press had to be used for a considerable quantity of grapes, it was drawn off into big earthenware jars. The new wine was not ready for drinking for at least forty days, by which time the stalks and skins swimming in it had settled down into a muddy deposit. This sediment was known as the "lees" and an interesting passage in the book of Jeremiah suggests that the wine was separated from the lees by being poured from one jar to another: "Moab has been at ease from his youth, and he has settled on his lees, and has not been emptied from vessel to vessel . . . therefore his taste remains in him, and his bouquet is not changed" (48. 11). The last comment implies a warning that wine needs to be kept relatively undisturbed and that too much pouring will set up reactions and turn it into vinegar. When the wine had been sufficiently strained, it was stored either in large eathernware jars, of which the lids were sealed with pitch or wax, or in well-tied wineskins.

The production of wine for daily use was by far the most important purpose of vine-growing, but there were various by-products which deserve to be mentioned. Some of the fresh grapes were dried in the sun to make raisins, which were highly prized, especially by soldiers and other travellers. In addition, it is almost certain that the Israelites made the thick golden substance (like maple molasses), which is known in the East as "dibs". It is intensely sweet and is produced by boiling the fresh grape juice repeatedly according to a recipe which demands perfect timing. It must have provided a welcome relief to the dullness of dry barley bread.

OLIVES

The gnarled and straggling olive-tree, its dark green foliage beautifully offset by the silver sheen on the underside of its leaves, was and is one of the most characteristic features of the Palestinian countryside. Once established, it yields a profitable crop of fruit even on parched and stony ground(51) with little cultivation beyond pruning, although the time it takes to settle down and develop its full yield may be anything up to fifteen years.

48   An Olive-Mill for pulping the fruit

The olive harvest came last in the season (about October–
November) after the grape-gathering had ended. Virtually
the whole crop was processed for its invaluable oil.

The finest quality was the "beaten oil" which was used in
the Temple. This was obtained from berries picked before they
were fully ripe and then gently pounded in an ordinary stone
mortar. It was meticulously decanted to remove every trace
of impurity. For general purposes, however, more wholesale
methods were adopted. The ripe olives were beaten from the
trees with a long pole, collected in reed or wicker baskets and
carried (by asses if necessary) to the place where they were to be
processed. The simplest method was to express the oil by
treading the fruit with the bare feet, in the same way (and
probably in the same press) as the grapes earlier in the season
(47). There can be little doubt, however, that before the end
of the period, oil-mills had to some extent superseded this
primitive foot-work. It is not easy to be confident about the
details of their construction nor about the date at which they
came into general use, but the simple mill shown in the illustration (48) is unlikely to be very wide of the mark. It consisted
of a circular stone basin eight feet or so in diameter, in which was
fitted a vertical mill-stone, so that it could revolve round a
central pivot. The mill-stone was turned by two people pushing
a long beam as they walked round and round the basin. In this

way, the olives were bruised and some of their oil was squeezed out and drawn off into vats or jars. The pulp which was left in the basin still contained a quantity of oil and so it was packed into baskets and taken to the presses.

49   An Olive-Press for extracting the oil

Like the mill, the oil-press(49) used in Old Testament times has to be reconstructed from later evidence. Its main feature was a wooden beam, of which the lower end was wedged into a hole in the vertical face of a rock (or, perhaps, slotted into a wooden frame) and the upper end weighted with big stones. The beam rested, at a point near its lower end, on a pile of two or three baskets of olive-pulp, which stood on a stone "table". As the oil dripped down under the pressure of the beam, it was collected in adjacent basins hewn out of the rock.

Great care was taken to purify the oil by allowing it to settle in vats; it may sometimes also have been treated with hot water. After it had been properly refined, it was stored in the usual large jars and skins, until it was needed for cooking, for toilet and medicinal purposes, or as fuel for lamps.

FIGS

Fig-trees were to be found in every corner of Palestine, in small groups at the edge of vineyards, or tucked away singly in isolated crannies. They needed little looking after and possessed the great advantage of bearing two or even three crops a year. As soon as the latter rains of winter were over, the green knobs began to appear on the naked and sprawling branches before ever any leaves came out. Most of this crop soon fell to the ground, but such fruit as did survive ripened about June into the delicacy which the Old Testament writers call the "firstripe fig". The second and biggest crop of the year was ready for eating by August or September and, in exceptional cases, more fruit appeared in the autumn.

Most of the figs were plucked for immediate eating and were as much a part of everyday diet in summer as tomatoes are

50   The mound of Megiddo—an Israelite city and
its agricultural "suburbs"

51   A Village in the stony hill-country of Judah, with an olive-tree
in the foreground

52 The Cedars of Lebanon

53 The Goats of Lebanon

with us. Some of the season's crop, however, was preserved in pressed cakes, which became very hard and, therefore, useful for packed meals. The most curious use made of figs was medicinal, as when Isaiah prescribed them as a poultice for Hezekiah's boil (see p. 193).

OTHER FRUIT AND VEGETABLES

The Israelites were not gardeners in our sense of the word, because only in exceptional circumstances was there a water-supply adequate for growing a variety of crops. Fruit-trees flourished better than anything else. The sycomore, for example, produced an abundant supply of bitter and indigestible figs, which were eaten by people who could afford nothing better. When the prophet Amos described himself as a "dresser of sycomore trees" (7. 14), he was making a reference to the practice of scratching the unripe sycomore fig to help it mature quickly. The almond-tree was another and much more attractive feature of the Palestinian scene, getting its name from the fact that it was the first of all the trees to wake up in the spring after its winter sleep (hence the word-play in Jeremiah 1. 11f.). The vivid scarlet blossom of the pomegranate came out soon after that of the almond and the juice of its ripe fruit was the Israelites' favourite soft drink in the hot summer months(34). The Old Testament frequently mentions the palm-tree, but is strangely silent about its dates; the same is true of the mulberry-tree, although it is difficult to believe that both dates and mulberries were quite unknown. It appears to be established, however, that Palestine had not yet been introduced to oranges and lemons, which are now one of the country's chief agricultural exports, and that the fruit usually translated in Old Testament passages as "apple" was certainly not the apple with which we are familiar. Favourite speculations identify it variously as the quince or the apricot.

Only the houses of the nobility enjoyed the amenity of a kitchen-garden. The attempt of the notorious Jezebel to seize Naboth's vineyard for such a "garden of herbs" is the subject of one of the Old Testament's most vigorous and revealing stories (I Kings 21). It is unlikely that Jezebel had it in mind to grow lentils and beans, which the poorer people used for their stews and (sometimes) their bread. More probably, she wanted to have a plentiful supply of such vegetables as melons, cucumbers, leeks, onions and garlic and the various aromatic plants, which her cooks would need for flavouring dishes in the royal kitchens.

CATTLE-BREEDING

When the Israelites became settled agriculturalists, they by no means abandoned their flocks and herds. They practised what we call "mixed farming", combining the cultivation of the land with the breeding of cattle. In the Old Testament, "cattle" is a portmanteau term which includes sheep, goats, oxen and asses and its original meaning ("possessions") is a reminder of Israel's early days in the wilderness, when sheep and goats were the only form of wealth.

During this period, shepherds maintained their high status in the social scale and their work continued as it had done for centuries (see pp. 48–51). In the new settled conditions, however, it was possible to breed animals which could not have survived the rigours of the wilderness. Now, for example, where the pasturage was sufficiently plentiful, oxen were reared and even poor farmers usually possessed at least one ox for use as a draught animal. The Hebrews, however, did not become a nation of beef-eaters and it was only among wealthy cattle-owners that choice young animals were withdrawn from the herd, kept in stalls and fattened up on special fodder for the table. The prophet Amos castigated this practice as a degenerate luxury (6. 4).

Another new animal bred by the Israelites after the settlement was the camel (the single-humped variety), which is now thought to have been domesticated in Palestine about 1000 B.C. It is unlikely that the average farmer was able to afford to keep camels among his herds, but their speed, long life, and capacity for going without food for days on end made them admirable beasts of burden for traders, despite their invincible stupidity and capricious temper. For ordinary farm work, the loyal, modest and indispensable ass remained supreme, since throughout this period horses continued to be almost entirely monopolized by the chariot divisions of the army.

HUNTING

Because of the diversity of its climate, Palestine had a wide variety of wild animals and one would naturally expect evidence

112

54   An Assyrian hunting scene

that the Israelites were keen huntsmen. That is not what we find in the Old Testament. Wild animals are certainly mentioned and references to hunting appear indirectly, but scenes of the chase are never described. This is the more remarkable in view of the fact that hunting was a popular sport both in Egypt and Assyria(54). The Assyrian reliefs depict the king's skill and daring in the lion hunt with a frequency which becomes almost monotonous. The royal gamekeepers even went to the trouble and expense of importing lions from Africa, because they were more formidable than the Syrian breed, and, therefore, more worthy of the king's prowess.

It is usual to conclude that the Israelites did not enjoy hunting like their neighbours and that their only interest in wild animals was to keep them away from their flocks and fields and to kill them for food. This conclusion may well be correct, but in this matter, as in others which concern popular recreations, it is possible that our lack of evidence owes at least something to a lack of interest on the part of the scribes from whom we have received the Old Testament. We are to a very large extent dependent on the information which they have supplied and from what we know of their outlook, it would not be at all surprising if they had simply omitted the things

113

they regarded with disfavour. Even though hunting was not so highly organized in Israel as it was in Assyria, and even though it was not the sport of kings, it is difficult to believe, on general grounds, that the men (and particularly the young men) of Palestine were never infected by the excitement of the chase.

The wild beasts for which the shepherd had to be always on the watch were the lion, bear, leopard, wolf, jackal, fox and possibly the hyena (for that is the meaning of the place-name Zeboim). The Syrian breed of lion, which is now extinct, was not in the least like our conventional idea of the King of Beasts(9) and was, apparently, less feared than the bear. Both were attacked, however, with a simple club. But more often they were snared in pits, which had been camouflaged with nets or light matting. Of the game of Palestine, three varieties "harts, and gazelles, and roebucks"(11) appear on Solomon's daily menu (I Kings 4. 23) and so we may take it that they were hunted regularly. Presumably, bows and slings were used and an Israelite hunting party must have looked very much like the Assyrian group illustrated(54). The Assyrians and the Egyptians used hounds in the chase, but this possibility must be excluded for the Israelites, since all the Old Testament references to dogs suggest only the despicable and vagrant scavenger.

Nets and snares of various kinds were also extensively employed, especially for fowling. Birds of the pigeon family, partridge and quail were all caught for food. Of the various kinds of net (the flight-net, the poachers' drag-net, the loose bag-net and so on), the so-called "clap-net" was the most popular among the Egyptians and probably also in Palestine. This was about four yards long and two yards wide and could be closed quickly by pulling on a rope at a given signal. The most common form of bird-snare consisted of a springy twig stuck in the ground with a noose attached to the free end. This was bent over and lightly fixed, so that it sprang up at a touch and drew the noose tight round the legs or body of its victim in the same movement as it tossed it into the air. The "fatted fowl" of Solomon's menu has usually been taken to refer to wild geese, which were trapped and then fattened for the table in Egypt. It now seems more probable that cuckoos are meant and that the Hebrew word is intended to imitate the bird's characteristic call!

FISHING

The Israelites knew so little about fishing that they were content to use one and the same word for the tiniest tiddler and the "great fish" which the story says swallowed Jonah (the "whale", incidentally, is a later invention). Being essentially land-locked, they knew nothing about the fish of the Mediterranean, and the Sea of Galilee, which supplies the fishing background of so much of the gospels, was on the very northern borders of Israel and during this period relatively unimportant. Apart from the Jordan, in which fish flourish until they are killed off by the chemicals of the Dead Sea, there are few rivers or inland lakes to turn the Israelite into a "compleat angler".

Fishing was certainly not a sport among the Hebrews (as it was among their Egyptian neighbours), although a few scattered Old Testament references prove that it was indulged in to a modest extent for food. A single verse in Habakkuk, metaphorically describing the wicked man as fishing, summarizes three different and familiar methods: "He taketh up all of them with the angle, he catcheth them in his net, and gathereth them in his drag" (1. 15). Angling with hook and line (but without rod—there was no fly-fishing) is the first method; the second uses the small weighted net, which is whirled round so that it enters the water in the shape of a tent and takes the fish by surprise; and the third method employs a drag-net, equipped with floats and weights, so that it moves through the water in a vertical position, bringing the fish either to a boat or to the edge of the water, in a diminishing circle.

The practice of spearing fish does not seem to have been used in this period and so the Israelites did not share the pleasure of harpooning parties, which the Egyptian sportsman (accompanied by his servants, favourite wife and hunting cat) seems to have much enjoyed.

Chapter VI

INDUSTRIAL LIFE

THE conventional picture of Old Testament life has for so long been monopolized by sheep-breeding and farming that the incongruity of implying a connexion between some of its trades and the industries of the twentieth century may be excused as a means of redressing the balance. By modern standards, Israelite industries were in their infancy—veritable babes in arms, but many of them, nevertheless, had ceased to be merely one-man businesses and homely crafts carried on in the domestic circle. Trade guilds had already started and cheap goods of a standard pattern were being turned out by primitive mass-production methods. Both the mining industry and building trade were demanding vast labour forces as early as the reign of Solomon, and the institution of slavery which supplied the need began, even at this early date, to provoke penetrating criticism from Israel's religious leaders. The vivid stories of Genesis are still, probably, the most familiar parts of the Old Testament, but their patriarchal simplicity is by no means representative of everyday life in Israel between the Exodus and the Exile.

TEXTILE WORKERS

There is little direct evidence in the Old Testament to indicate that spinning and weaving had developed beyond the home circle. We hear, for example, of the virtuous housewife with a spindle in her hands (Proverbs 31. 19) and of Delilah, who wove the seven locks of the unfortunate Samson into a piece of cloth being made on a nearby hand-loom (Judges 16. 13). Such references are exactly what we should have expected. What we could hardly have anticipated is the recent discovery of archaeologists that spinning, weaving and dyeing were concentrated in certain Israelite towns during the period in a way which properly earns them the title of industrial centres. In two or three ancient cities, notably Debir, basketfuls of loom weights have been excavated in close proximity to apparatus for dyeing. In Debir, for example, it is estimated that there

116

must have been no fewer than twenty to forty dyeing installations, and it is safe to assume that there was a flourishing local industry, exploiting both the extensive sheep-farming of the region and the opportunity for selling woollen goods to merchants travelling on the main trade-route from Egypt to the north.

Of the raw material used for textiles, sheep's wool was the chief. Although there are considerable gaps in our knowledge, it is nevertheless possible to reconstruct in broad outline the whole process of manufacture from the animal's back to the finished garment.

Sheep-shearing in Palestine was always a great social and religious occasion, but otherwise it must have differed little from what may still be seen on many an English farm. First of all, the sheep were well "dipped" in a pool to clean their fleece; then they were sheared. After the shearing, the wool was washed a second time to remove grease and to produce that beautiful whiteness with which the writer of the Song of Songs had the courage to compare his beloved's teeth! (4. 2). It was then combed or "carded" and got ready for spinning.

Before the invention of the spinning-wheel in the sixteenth century A.D., all spinning was done on a simple hand spindle. No Israelite specimens have survived, but a considerable number of spindle "whorls" have been unearthed. These were made of stone, clay or bone and their purpose was to weight the spindle shaft and give it momentum. The spindle itself consisted of a thin wooden stick about a foot long; it had a notch at the top and was stuck through a whorl so that the weight came in the lower half. To do her work, the spinster held the strands of combed wool in her left hand, or under her left arm, and with her right hand drew out enough to twist into a yarn between her thumb and forefinger. She attached this yarn to the notch of her spindle, gave it a sharp twist, and then let it fall in front of her. As it fell, it gave a twist to the thread and when it got near the ground, she stopped it and wound the thread on to the spindle shaft. Hebrew women repeated this operation as easily as the modern woman does her knitting, talking or even walking meanwhile. The art of spinning seems to have been brought to the pitch of perfection in Egypt, and examples of it still survive in the pieces of fine linen woven for the mummification of kings. The thread of this material is of an amazing fineness; it has, indeed, been calculated that about sixty miles of it would weigh only a pound.

The Egyptians also led the ancient world in the allied art of weaving. Their tomb paintings help us recreate a sketch of the Hebrew weaver's tools and methods from the scattered and vague Old Testament references. The most primitive form of weaving was little more than plaiting, and no doubt in the backwoods of Israel such crude methods were practised during our period. The two sets of thread with which a weaver works are called the "warp" and the "weft", the warp being that which runs the length of the cloth and the weft that which goes across the piece, under and over the warp. When the warp was fixed to some kind of frame, it may be said that the earliest loom came into being.

Ancient looms were of two kinds—horizontal and vertical. The horizontal loom was pegged out on the ground and the weaver had to crouch at his work(56). It is this stooping position which enables us to identify certain Egyptian pictures of the loom as being of the *horizontal* type, despite the fact that the artist's curious perspective makes the loom appear to be vertical(55). The most primitive kind of *vertical* loom consisted of a top beam from which the warp threads were suspended and kept taut by means of loom weights, looking rather like pierced doughnuts. In this case, the weaver stood to work and started his web from the top.

In every kind of loom, the main problem is the separation of the warp threads into two sets(56), so that a passage (or "shed") can be made for the insertion of the weft (C). Weaving requires at least two of these "sheds", so that a weft thread which has just passed *under* one set of warp threads may, on its return journey across the cloth, go *over* the same threads. The making of the first "shed" provided no real

55 Egyptian Women crouching to weave at a horizontal loom

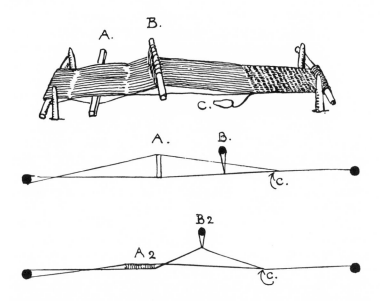

56   A simple horizontal Loom with diagrams to illustrate the first and second "sheds", showing (A) the "shed-stick", (B) the "leash-rod", (C) the bobbin of weft thread

difficulty. Instead of threading the weft under and over the warp by hand (as in darning), the ancients soon discovered how to use a flat stick (like a long ruler) (A), which was kept in position across the warp under every alternate thread. When it was turned on its edge, it separated the warp into the required two sets of threads and made a passage for the weft. It was the problem of arranging the *second* "shed", when the position of each warp thread had to be reversed, which exercised the ingenuity of the craftsman. Obviously, a second stick could not be inserted like the first and left in position. It is probable that for a long time every *second* weft thread was laboriously passed under and over the warp by hand. It was, therefore, an enormous step forward when some ingenious person thought of attaching alternate warp threads (those which went *under* the first stick) to a second stick by means of loops of thread. This is called the leash-rod (B). So long as it remained lying on the warp between the edge of the cloth and the first stick,

119

the threads which were attached to it remained in the "down" position and the weft passed over them when the first "shed" was made by the first stick. When, however, the leash-rod was pulled up vertically from the warp (B²), it brought the lower threads to the top and a second "shed" was made. Thus the stick and the leash-rod were used alternately.

It is impossible to determine exactly what stage had been reached in the development of the loom in Old Testament times. From the excavated loom weights, it is clear that the Israelites used some type of vertical loom and this deduction is confirmed by the discovery of the charred remains of a heavy upright beam in a weaver's shop at Lachish. On the other hand, it is virtually certain that the loom on which Delilah wove Samson's hair was of the horizontal type. It is fair to conclude, therefore, that both types were used in different places in the period and it is even possible that a hybrid type was used, in which the warp was set at an angle and stretched from the ground to a beam fixed high on the opposite wall of the weaver's room. If we may judge by the reference in Job 7. 6—"My days are swifter than a weaver's shuttle", the leash-rod had been invented and was in use not long after the Exile, since otherwise the suggestion of speed here would be difficult to explain. This, incidentally, is the only Old Testament reference to the shuttle—a wooden boat-shaped object containing a bobbin of weft thread. Previously, the weft thread was poked across the warp with a forked stick.

Some scholars identify the "weaver's beam" of the Old Testament with the leash-rod, but it is more likely to refer to one of the heavy beams of the vertical loom. It has already been pointed out that a top beam from which the warp was suspended formed part of the most primitive vertical loom, but as time went on a second beam was fixed to the bottom of the loom instead of the inconvenient weights. Eventually, it was seen that if this bottom beam were made to rotate, the cloth could be rolled on to it as it was woven. The two-fold advantage of this rotating beam were that cloth could be woven of any length desired and the weaver could remain sitting in front of his loom with the edge of the web always within reach.

The initial setting up of the loom must have been the heaviest and most exciting part of the work, and Old Testament writers refer to it in metaphors to suggest the beginning of some

120

important venture. Whereas spinning was done exclusively by women, weaving employed men as well; it must, indeed, have been hard and tedious work.

Woollen textiles predominated, but goats' hair and camels' hair were used for coarser cloths—to be made up into tents, bags, "sackcloth" and heavy cloaks for shepherds. In so far as the strict letter of the Law was obeyed, wool and linen were never woven together, according to a curious prohibition which had its origin in primitive religion.

Linen was manufactured from flax, which (as the Gezer Calendar proves) was grown in Palestine (see p. 98). When the flax stalks were ready for gathering, they were pulled up by the roots and beaten with sticks to free them from their seed pods. They were then dried in the sun (often on the roof-top, as in Joshua 2. 6), after which they were steeped for a week or so in water to separate the inner fibres from the woody part of the stalk. This process is known as "retting". After they had been dried and beaten a second time, the stalks were sorted and combed before spinning. The "fine linen" of Egypt was considered a great luxury and it is probable that the Israelites imported it for special purposes, such as Temple vestments. Their own product was much coarser, as we may now see for ourselves from a specimen which was recently discovered with the Dead Sea Scrolls.

The Hebrews were not restricted to the natural colour of their raw materials; as the excavated sites testify, they practised dyeing on an extensive scale. Their dye-plants appear to have been built on a fairly standard plan, and included as their main piece of equipment a number of substantial vats made out of solid blocks of stone. They look rather like up-ended garden-rollers, about a yard in height and the same in diameter (57). They were hollowed out at the top into a basin with a narrow mouth (about six inches across) and, near the edge of the vat, a deep channel was cut all round and pierced at one point to make a drain into the basin. The drain was to allow surplus dye, which was spilled in extracting the thread from the basin, to drip back again. It was too valuable for a drop to be wasted. Near these vats, other remains of the dyeing industry have been found, such as jars containing slaked lime and decomposed potash and various stone basins and water cisterns. To judge by the small size of the basin-mouth in all the vats, it appears

57 Stone Dye-vat and Basin

that the thread was dyed before weaving, and not the cloth in the piece.

From the Old Testament evidence, it is difficult to avoid the conclusion that the Hebrews did not possess any highly developed sense of colour. Their language, for example, has no single word for colour, and their words for describing the various colours and shades of colours are so few that they cannot have been used much in general conversation. Even such obvious colours as blue and yellow do not occur as distinct terms, although, perhaps, we ought to make allowances for the fact that the Old Testament books were written by men and not women!

Of the colours produced by the use of pigments, scarlet and purple are the most frequently mentioned. Scarlet dye was produced from an insect which lived on a particular kind of tree (like the cochineal-insect which is parasitic on the cactus plant). When it was crushed and put into hot water, it produced a vivid red liquid. This dye-stuff was used, among other things, for the hangings and furniture of the priestly tabernacle, and its glaring and indelible character may be judged from the fact that Isaiah referred to it in describing the sins of his contemporaries (1. 18).

Purple, however, was the most highly-prized of all the dyes. It was obtained from a shell-fish (*murex brandaris* and *murex trunculus*) which was caught in large quantities off the Phoenician coast round Tyre. Hence, the familiar name "Tyrian purple". This dye was so famous that it gave its name to Syria and Palestine, for "Canaan" probably meant originally the "Land of the Purple". The Greeks called the Canaanites "Phoenicians", from their own word for purple. To make this precious fluid, the top of the shell-fish was cut off and the yellowish secretion collected. It contained two ingredients, one a dark blue and the other a brilliant red. According to the species of fish, the colour it produced in the process of dyeing was either a purple-blue (called "blue" in the Old Testament) or a purple-red (called "purple"). Presumably, experience enabled the craftsmen to produce many intermediate shades.

58　Household pottery from the Southern Kingdom

59　Terracotta jugs from the Northern Kingdom, showing the refinement of Phoenician influence in form and finish and a Canaanite figurine from the Northern Kingdom

POTTERY

60 The Gezer Calendar
(*see p.* 98 *and p.* 179)

61 Small bronze stand from
Megiddo (*see p.* 127)

62 The Underground Tunnel of
the Megiddo waterworks
(*see pp.* 139 *ff.*)

63 Horned Incense Altar made of
limestone (*see p.* 232)

As it is very unlikely that dyeing in purple was practised by the Israelites, they had to import all their purple goods. It is, therefore, not surprising that "to be born in the purple" implies wealth and rank.

We may take it, however, that native workers knew how to produce scarlet dye and that they learnt how to use vegetable dyes like almond (for yellow) and madder (for red). At least this degree of proficiency becomes the more likely when we take into account their knowledge of chemicals for cleaning raw materials. For example, we read in Jeremiah 2. 22: "For though thou wash thee with lye [that is, natron or nitre], and take thee much soap [that is, some alkaline salt], yet thine iniquity is marked before me." The Hebrews clearly had a rudimentary form of liquid soap, and they almost certainly possessed more mineral dyes than we are now able to trace.

METAL WORKERS

The Israelite metal worker is still something of a mystery. The Old Testament includes a fairly technical description of the dangerous job of a miner in Job 28. 1–11, but it never directly portrays the smith at work in his shop. We have to be content with a number of metaphorical references drawn from metal working (such as the description of smelting in Ezekiel 22. 17–22), but these are enough to indicate that it was part and parcel of the everyday scene. There is enough evidence to show that the Israelite smith had learnt to use bellows for his furnace, that he knew how to cast small objects in gold, silver and copper, and that he could hammer metal into sheets, solder, weld and polish.

Probably the most familiar kind of metal worker in the small towns and villages of our period was the successor of the early travelling tinker, who went on his rounds, carrying his equipment on the back of an ass and stopping to make small tools and repair metal utensils on the spot. It has already been suggested (p. 48) that the Egyptian tomb painting of Beni-Hasan portrays a group of tinkers with their portable goat-skin bellows. Perhaps in Palestine, as in Greece, such travelling tinkers eked out their livelihood by music and fortune-telling, like the gipsies who are still to be seen on fair-grounds today.

This, however, is less than half the story of metal working in Old Testament times. In the last twenty years, a number of extraordinarily illuminating archaeological expeditions have brought to light the existence of a highly-organized metal industry in the Arabah, the desert region on the southern border of Palestine between the Dead Sea and the Red Sea, occupied by the Edomites. The centre of this industry was Ezion-geber, Solomon's naval base on the Red Sea. Nelson Glueck has now established that Solomon deliberately planned and built this city as a huge factory site, the greatest ever discovered in the ancient Near East and approximating more closely to Birmingham or Sheffield than any other Old Testament city. This vast industrial centre was the hub of Solomon's extensive trade in copper and iron, which he exported in exchange for the gold of Ophir (see pp. 172 f.).

From this new evidence, it is possible to reconstruct a good deal about the nature and extent of the Israelites' development of the metal industry. Simple furnaces have been discovered near the mines of the Arabah, in which the crude copper ore was first roughly "roasted", before being transported to refining centres like Ezion-geber. Here it was finally processed and made into ingots and, perhaps, various kinds of metal goods. The elaborate smelteries in and around the city show how ingeniously the prevailing winds from the north were exploited to give the necessary draught to the furnaces and there is little doubt that the wooded slopes of the region supplied the necessary charcoal.

These discoveries in Edom are a startling revelation. They help explain where some of Solomon's wealth came from for the fabulous buildings of Jerusalem. They show why the policy of the early kings of Israel was so much concerned with the winning and retention of the land of Edom. They also illuminate the description of Palestine as "a land whose stones are iron, and out of whose hills thou mayest dig copper" (Deuteronomy 8. 9), which, in view of the absence of mines west of the Jordan, has always been puzzling. Many other problems, however, remain unsolved. We do not know, for example, where the metal workers of Israel obtained the tin necessary for alloys like bronze, which is a mixture of copper and tin; it is possible (but by no means certain) that from about the tenth century B.C., the Phoenicians were importing it from the West. Again, we should like to know much more about the technical processes used by Solomon's miners and refinery workers, and the extent to which they depended on foreign experts. Phoenician metal workers, for example, were responsible for the work in Solomon's Temple and are said to have done their bronze casting in clay moulds on the east side of the Jordan (I Kings 7. 46). It has been doubted whether the metallurgical science of the period was equal to casting such immense pieces as the Temple pillars (see pp. 224f.), although we possess clear evidence that even the Israelites were capable of casting such complicated objects as the bronze stand found at Megiddo(61). Its four open-work panels show an offering being made to an enthroned goddess and the detail is remarkable considering the fact that the complete stand is only about 3½ inches high. Any reliable estimate of the technical competence of both Phoenician and Israelite metal workers must await further evidence from the archaeologists.

The development of Ezion-geber followed hard on the heels of the general adoption of iron weapons and implements in Palestine; and the discovery of iron as well as copper deposits in the Arabah region must have stimulated it. Roughly speaking, the Israelite conquest of Palestine coincided with the transition from the Bronze Age to the Iron Age, and at first the Hebrew invaders were greatly handicapped by the fact that their enemies possessed iron weapons and they were without them. It is said, for example, that the God of the Hebrews "could not drive out the inhabitants of the valley, because they had chariots of iron" (Judges 1. 19). These iron-clad chariots gave the Canaanites military supremacy in flat country, with the result that Israelite successes were confined to the hills. Later, in the time of Samuel, it was the Philistines who held a monopoly in iron production and jealously guarded its technical secrets. The revealing statement of I Samuel 13. 19–21 shows how they denied the Israelites iron weapons and how they exploited their monopoly when the service of metal workers was required for agricultural implements(64). Professor G. E. Wright has retranslated the passage as follows:

> Now there was no smith found throughout all the land of Israel, for the Philistines said: "(There must be none) lest the Hebrews make sword or spear". And all Israel went down to the Philistines for each man to sharpen his plough-point and his axe and his adze and his mattock (?). And the price was a pim [two-thirds of a shekel] for the mattocks (or plough-points?) and for the axes, and

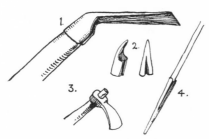

64   Iron Tools: 1. Mattock; 2. Plough-points; 3. Adze; 4. Ox-goad

a third of a shekel for sharpening the adzes and for setting (or straightening) the goads.[1]

The Philistines had learnt how to make iron weapons in the twelfth century B.C., but it was only when their power was broken under Saul and David that their secret became public property and iron goods were released for the Israelites.

Little by little, iron displaced flint for sickles and it came into general use for spearheads, chisels, awls, pick-axes, mason's hammers, tips of ox-goads, pruning knives, forks, fish-hooks, cooking utensils and a hundred and one small metal articles (65–7). Before this development, bronze was the hardest metal for daily use, since meteoric iron, which contained a small quantity of nickel, was regarded as a semi-precious metal suitable only for jewellery and expensive gifts. Iron was cheaper than bronze and so once it was introduced, it became popular fairly quickly.

Neither silver nor gold was mined in Palestine. Both were imported on a large scale, the former being used extensively as a medium of exchange even before the invention of minted money and the latter for such luxurious ornamentation as Solomon loved.

Between the simple tinker and the technicians of an industrial plant like that of Ezion-geber, there is a wide gulf. We can only guess what kind of local smith supplied the farmer and carpenter with nails and tools, the soldier with weapons and the housewife with pans, needles and pins (the latter including *safety*-pins!). It is probable that the smiths worked in family businesses, like the potters, and formed themselves into trade guilds. At least, they

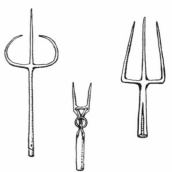

65–7   Types of Metal Fork

[1] *The Biblical Archaeologist*, May 1943.

acquired a sufficient importance in Hebrew society to be ranked with the leading men deported by Babylon in the last years of the Southern Kingdom (Jeremiah 24. 1).

Pottery is as difficult to destroy as it is easy to break. We have, therefore, more direct evidence of the potter's craft than of any other in Old Testament times. It has provided the archaeologist with an invaluable clue for dating the various levels or "strata" of excavated sites. Indeed, digging in Palestine has unearthed pottery as old as any known in the world.

The pottery of the period is not for the connoisseur. Fine hand-made ware of delicate design and exquisite workmanship had been produced in Palestine at an earlier period, but the potter's art fell on evil days with the arrival of the Israelites. The potters of the Old Testament were men who turned out everyday articles for everyday use. Indeed, "turned out" is the right word, for the fast-spinning potter's wheel had already given rise to mass-production methods.

Few jars and jugs were shaped laboriously by hand; most were "thrown" on the wheel(116). This wheel was fixed to the top of a spindle which ran through the centre of another wheel below. The lower wheel was heavier to give momentum as the potter spun it by hand. There is no evidence before about 200 B.C. that the Jews used a mechanism for operating the wheel by foot.

To increase the output, various mass-production methods were devised. For instance, sometimes a great cone of clay would be worked on the wheel at one time and articles shaped and "pinched off" from the top until it was all used up. Standardized shapes and sizes were fixed, so that the various stages of manufacture could be divided between different workers. Apprentices, for example, were set to making handles for jars (indeed, their inexpert fingers have left traces which are still visible), or they were made to rough out articles which were then handed to skilled craftsmen to finish. Such methods would be easier to follow when several potters worked together in a family or a guild, and there is evidence to show that such co-operative enterprise was practised in the period and that the various groups even stamped their goods with their own trade-mark.

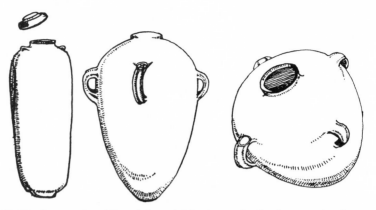

68–70 Pottery Jars (*from left to right*): storage jar for documents; storage jar for wine and oil; jar showing stamped handle (*see* pp. 167f.)

The clay used by the Israelite potter was usually a red variety taken from just below the surface of the soil. Before it was ready for working on the wheel, it had to be left to be weathered by sun, rain and frost, which helped to break it up and rid it of chemical impurities. It was then kneaded by treading and, if clay of a better quality was required, filtered in large vats. Special clay was needed for articles with particular uses. Cooking-pots, for example, which had to withstand heat, were made from a clay to which crushed limestone had been added. In any case, after the vessel had been shaped on the wheel, it was allowed to dry until it had become about as hard as leather. It was then returned to the wheel and shaped further with a cutting tool. Finally, the vessel was baked in a furnace.

71, 72 Scent Bottles

In one potter's workshop, discovered in a cave at Lachish, many sherds were found which had clearly been used as tools for rubbing the leather-hard clay. This process of "burnishing" made the surface shine after firing. Glazing was still unknown, but sometimes articles were given a coating (or "slip") of fine

130

clay before they were sent to the furnace. Otherwise, there was little decoration.

The bulk of the potter's output was intended for domestic use and consisted chiefly of jugs, pitchers, cups, storage jars, water-decanters and oil-decanters(25, 58, 59, 69). A curious fact which throws light on Hebrew table manners is that very few plates have been discovered. The potter also supplied every house with its lamp(23), children with their toys (see p. 80), and business men with jars for the safe-keeping of their contracts(68). He also produced more delicate articles, such as small scent bottles shaped like miniature jugs(71, 72), ointment jars and cheap jewellery. Not least, he made objects for religious use, like the figurines, of which so many examples have now been unearthed(59, 117). It is evident, on examination, that the heads of these figures were made in standard moulds of clay or metal (attention being paid to the features only) and that they were then fixed to the body or pedestal, by means of a wooden peg. They were very good specimens of early mass-production to meet a heavy popular demand.

Despite the inferiority of Israelite pottery when compared with the high order of design and craftsmanship of an earlier period, experts hold the opinion that the potters of Old Testament times achieved a better standard of workmanship than that of modern commercial ware.

BRICK-MAKERS

It is very strange that we hear so little of brick-makers from the writers of the Old Testament. They must have been familiar and numerous, since in Palestine, as elsewhere in the East, bricks were the commonest of building materials. It is also strange at first sight that bricks should have been so largely used in a country where so much building stone was readily available, but this preference is easily explained by the scarcity of metal tools suitable for cutting and dressing stone.

Popular notions of Israelite brick-making have been much confused by the proverbial saying about "bricks without straw", which takes its origin from a misunderstanding of the story of the captive Hebrews in Egypt (Exodus 5). The point of this narrative is that Pharaoh decided to withhold the usual straw he had been supplying for the manufacture of bricks in order to force the Hebrews to find it themselves: "Thus saith Pharaoh,

I will not give you straw. Go yourselves, get you straw where ye can find it: for nought of your work shall be diminished. So the people were scattered abroad throughout all the land of Egypt to gather stubble for straw" (Exodus 5. 10f.). It is now an established fact that nearly all mud-bricks of the type most commonly used in the ancient East contained finely-chopped straw. It was added to the clay to strengthen it, on the same principle as modern builders reinforce their concrete with iron rods. It is said that a mud-brick reinforced with straw is no less than three times as strong as one made without it. Sometimes sand was used instead of straw and the Israelite bricks which have been examined contain all kinds of debris besides— like bits of pottery and small stones. A further advantage of straw is that, being vegetable matter, it sets up a chemical reaction and releases acids which have a strengthening effect on the mud.

Although we have so little direct evidence from the Old Testament about the methods followed by the Hebrew brick-maker, Egyptian sources are particularly illuminating and the makers of mud-bricks have been so conservative in their procedure even up to the present day, that we may safely assume that Egyptian evidence gives us an insight into Israelite practice. An Egyptian tomb painting of the fifteenth century B.C. illustrates the whole process(73), but when we examine it, we must remember that the impression it gives of the bricks being placed in piles is only the artist's method of representing perspective. They are actually being laid out in rows. The brick-makers depicted here are expressly described as slaves and as David also is said to have made his Ammonite captives labour at brick-making (II Samuel 12. 31), it is clear that the job was regarded as being particularly tough and fit for the slave class only.

First, the clay was mixed with water and chopped straw and then kneaded into the right consistency, either with a hoe (as in the painting) or (more commonly) with the feet. The man who actually made the bricks prepared the ground by sprinkling it with finely chopped straw or something else which would prevent the wet mud from sticking. When the damp clay was brought to him, he pressed it into a portable wooden mould the size of a single brick and then lifted the mould away by means of a wooden handle. The mould was then placed

73 Captives making Bricks (*From an Egyptian
tomb painting of the fifteenth century* B.C.)

immediately next to the newly-made brick and the procedure
was repeated until the whole brickyard was covered by bricks
neatly arranged in rows. The wet bricks were left for two or
three days to dry out a little, and it was presumably at this
stage of manufacture that stray dogs sometimes scampered
across them and left paw-prints which can still be detected.
Some bricks were officially stamped with a trade-mark, or
(as in Egypt) with the name of the king or the building for
which they were intended. The only other markings which
were made before the bricks dried out were ridges impressed
on the top with the fingers and these were intended to give a
better "key" to the mortar in building. After the preliminary
drying process, during which the bricks were turned to catch
the sun, they were loosely stacked in the open air and left
for another two or three weeks before being handed over to the
builder. In Mesopotamia, the first of the summer months,
corresponding to our May–June, was called "the month of
bricks", because the sun was then just right for drying the
mud.

The finished bricks varied in size, presumably in relation to
the particular building for which they were made, but, on the
average, they were much bigger than the ones with which we

133

are familiar and often measured as much as $21 \times 10 \times 4$ inches. It is said that modern brick-makers in the East, who follow the ancient methods, can turn out, with the help of a single mate, as many as two to three thousand bricks in a working day. What that means in terms of back-ache, it is painful to imagine.

There is very little evidence that the Israelites made kiln-baked bricks; the short description in Nahum 3. 14: "go into the clay, and tread the mortar, make strong the brickkiln" is properly corrected by the marginal reading of the Revised Version to "lay hold of the *brickmould*". The same correction of "brickkiln" to "brickmould" is made in II Samuel 12. 31, which, incidentally, refers not to David's torturing his prisoners, but to his putting them to servile labour. The reference in Nahum is part of the preparations to be made for a siege and so it recalls the remarkable fact that sun-dried mud-bricks were able to withstand an incredible amount of rough usage. Even Israelite fortifications were built of them and they were used throughout for Ezion-geber, Solomon's factory town on the Red Sea. It is here that a brickyard has been unearthed, with hundreds of half-finished and unused bricks still in position, as they have been for nearly three thousand years.

MASONS AND CARPENTERS

It is unlikely that the native Israelite building trade ever really flourished in this period. Its development was held up partly by the inadequacy of building tools, but much more by the poverty of the majority of city-dwellers. If there had been a sufficient number of customers requiring well-built houses, Israelite architects, masons and carpenters would, no doubt, have responded.

The fine buildings of Megiddo (16, 18, 104, 106) and Samaria, erected in prosperous times under royal patronage, were quite exceptional. Their style and probably the masons for their construction were borrowed from Phoenicia. We know that David and Solomon imported builders from Tyre (both masons and carpenters: II Samuel 5. 11; I Kings 5. 1–12, 18) and the extraordinarily interesting proto-Ionic capitals (5), which were discovered on the site of these two cities, were almost certainly the work of Phoenician craftsmen, from whom later the Greeks borrowed the style. How much the Israelites who worked alongside the foreign master-craftsmen learnt from them and to what extent they imitated their methods, we have no means of knowing. It has been suggested that after the Phoenician masons had completed the Temple at Jerusalem, they stayed at Megiddo on their way home and helped finish the king's buildings there. It would be unjust, however, to reject out of hand the possibility that the Tyrian craftsmen found some of the Israelites apt pupils and that their methods were continued after they had left the country.

To whomsoever the credit is due, there is no doubt that the builders of Megiddo and Samaria were highly skilled men. In building walls, for example, they knew the method of alternating stones laid across the width of the wall (called "headers") with stones laid lengthwise (called "stretchers")—a combination which gives great additional strength. They knew, too, how to economize (without weakening their building) by constructing corners and supports of carefully-dressed stone and filling in the intervening spaces with rubble(106). These corner-stones, which guaranteed strength and stability, became a figure of speech in Israel and are referred to in the Old Testament to describe "chiefs" or prominent men on whom the community relied for its well-being (see Judges 20. 2 and I Samuel 14. 38 and compare the marginal reading in the Revised Version). The masons were also careful about the foundations of their buildings and sometimes cut trenches for them out of the solid rock. The skill with which they dressed the edges of their blocks of stone was noted by the excavators of Megiddo and Samaria, who even found traces of red paint which had been used to ensure a correct alignment. The laying of the stones of the Great Gate of Megiddo(18) was so excellent that, although no mortar was used, even a thin knife could not be inserted between the blocks. It is doubtful whether Israelite masons ever achieved so high a standard. Nevertheless, considering that they had to work with inadequate tools (even allowing for the growing use of iron), it is remarkable that they progressed as far as the archaeological evidence suggests. Their success is to be accounted for partly by the softness of the native limestone. So long as it remained underground, the limestone rock was fairly easy to cut; it became hard only when it was exposed to the air. When limestone blocks were quarried locally (as nearly always happened), they were laid

135

in position quickly so that they welded together and dried out in a solid mass, very much like our own concrete. Extra strength was given to walls made of brick by various kinds of mortar, which had a clay base and was mixed with crushed limestone or straw. The outside surface of walls was often given a plaster wash, perhaps for appearance sake (as is suggested in Ezekiel 13. 10), but more often to protect them against the elements.

It was unusual to build houses entirely of stone; as Amos indignantly pointed out (5. 11), they were a great extravagance. In most buildings, both mud-bricks and wood were used. Characteristically, the lower part of a wall was built of stone and the upper part of brick and wood. For example, the wall of the courtyard in front of Solomon's temple is explicitly said to have had three courses of hewn stone and a course of cedar beams (I Kings 7. 12). The disadvantage of both brick and wood is that they are perishable, brick from damp and wood from fire. For this reason, excavators have been disappointed in their hope of finding intact the upper stories and the roofs of Israelite buildings.

All the information we possess makes it clear that masons and carpenters worked in the closest co-operation. When the local forests, which supplied the bulk of the timber, failed to produce beams long enough to support the roof of the larger kind of house, the masons adopted the method of building lines of pillars to reduce the span. The only alternative was to follow the extravagant precedent of Solomon and import cedars from Lebanon(52). The base of these pillars was usually a roughly-squared single stone and as this would be about five feet high and anything up to 3,000 pounds in weight, it was no easy job to get it from the quarry to the building site. Nevertheless, they were found in great quantities in the Megiddo stables (105) and in the eighth-century houses of Debir. Their use in private houses at Debir may owe something to the fact that it was a centre of the textile industry and vertical looms pulling on the walls of weaving rooms would demand something like pillars to take the extra strain.

The familiar horizontal lines of Old Testament buildings were unrelieved by any arches or vaulting. Hebrew architects had not yet mastered the structural problems involved and this is one of the reasons why even their big buildings had only the smallest slit windows. To "cut out windows" was an expensive business if you were to avoid weakening the masonry and it is condemned by Jeremiah as a refinement which only a heedlessly extravagant king would ever contemplate (Jeremiah 22. 14).

The work of the carpenter is inevitably more elusive than that of the mason, but he would obviously be in constant demand for dozens of jobs about the city (making and repairing the doors at the gate), the farm (threshing-sledges, carts, shafts for mattocks, ploughs, winnowing forks and so on), and the home (for which he made the ladders and furniture). One suspects, however, that much of this carpentry was done by the men of the household during the long winter months and that the professional was called in only for big structural jobs. Perhaps, therefore, it is not very strange that the Old Testament provides only one description of the carpenter at work and he is no ordinary joiner, but a Babylonian craftsman engaged in carving an idol: "The carpenter stretcheth out a line; he marketh it out with red chalk; he shapeth it with chisels, and he marketh it out with the divider, and shapeth it after the figure of a man" (Isaiah 44. 13). Presumably, the Israelite wood-carver used similar tools, although his skill was required only for panelling the sitting-rooms of the well-to-do.

HYDRAULIC ENGINEERS

One day in 1880, a boy from a junior technical school in Jerusalem was bathing in the pool of Siloam, when he suddenly came across an inscription a few yards away from the mouth of the tunnel through which the pool was supplied with water. This is what it read:

> This is the boring through. This is the story of the boring through: whilst the miners lifted the pick each towards his fellow and whilst three cubits yet remained to be bored through, there was heard the voice of a man calling his fellow, for there was a split in the rock on the right hand and on the left hand. And on the day of the boring through the miners struck, each in the direction of his fellow, pick against pick. And the water started flowing from the source to the pool twelve hundred cubits. A hundred cubits was the height of the rock above the heads of the miners.[1]

[1] The translation is taken from J. Simons, *Jerusalem in the Old Testament*.

This is a first-hand record of the crucial moment of one of the most amazing engineering triumphs of the Israelites in Old Testament times. The inscription (consisting of six lines of Hebrew of the kind which Isaiah wrote) was cut in the lower half of a panel prepared on the wall of the tunnel. If, as is possible, the upper half of the panel had been intended for an illustration of the boring operation, it is a great loss that the craftsman never completed his work. The brief record which was completed describes the finishing of a tunnel made just before 700 B.C. in the reign of Hezekiah of Judah to protect the water-supply of Jerusalem when the city was threatened by the Assyrians. In constructing it, two gangs of workmen had started from opposite ends, hacking their way through solid limestone rock, to make a conduit which would bring the water of the spring Gihon in the exposed valley of the Kidron to a point within the city's defences. On maintaining this water-supply, the security of the city very largely depended. After they had progressed from each end, covering between them about 580 yards, the two gangs were able to hear each other's pick-axes. It is not difficult to imagine the intense thrill of that moment. Those who have since explored and mapped out the tunnel tell us that in their excitement the miners lost some of their control; they zigzagged off course, became careless about the levels of the floor and ceiling, and failed to finish off the surface of the walls as well as they had done up to that time. Soon, they could hear the voices of their fellows and, at last, when the final breach was made, two grimy, sweating, but triumphant Israelites greeted each other through the hole. The Siloam Tunnel was complete.

It is reckoned that from start to finish the operation must have taken over six months—six months of labour in the most terrible conditions. The air-supply underground must have been extremely bad, as modern explorers (who have to come out for frequent "breathers") can testify. And in the eighth century B.C., the only light was the dim glow supplied by saucer lamps and torches, which still further exhausted the air-supply. A number of triangular notches which have been found in the walls of the tunnel at various points may well have served as lamp-brackets. It is quite astonishing that the miners, without any sort of scientific instruments or surveying methods to guide them, were able to keep their direction as well as they did.

Although they did lose some ground in making a large S-bend, the course they took is, nevertheless, under twice the length of the distance between the spring and the pool. The marks of the pick-axes may still be seen on the walls of the tunnel and it is evident that the workers were remarkably expert at handling them in so cramped a space. The narrowness of the tunnel made it impossible for more than one man to work at a time and though, for the most part, the height is about six feet, it is less in some places and much of the cutting must have been done in a stooping or a crouching position.

The Old Testament historians were duly impressed by this achievement and refer to it more than once (II Kings 20. 20; II Chronicles 32. 30), but it by no means stands alone. Centuries before David was king in Jerusalem, the old inhabitants of the city had taken comparable measures. Several shafts cut into the solid rock in pre-Israelite times have been excavated and it is plain that the intention of the early engineers was to reach the level of their spring and to be able to draw water from it without leaving the city's defences. In these early works, an underground corridor was constructed to connect with the main vertical shaft, from the top of which skin "buckets" could be let down into the basin below. There were no machines of any kind for drawing up the bucket-rope and so we can imagine what a business it must have been to get water for the population of the entire city.

It has been conjectured that this primitive installation is referred to in II Samuel 5. 8 and that David's forces actually captured the city by making their entry through the water conduit. It is more likely, however, that David's men seized control of the tunnel, blocked the water-supply and so. compelled the city to capitulate. It is hard to appreciate that these pre-Davidic shafts were cut before iron tools were available and that the workmen hacked out the rock with implements of flint and bronze.

Yet another system of waterworks built by Canaanite engineers before the Hebrew conquest has been discovered at Megiddo. Here a vertical shaft was bored through eighty feet of debris and limestone. This was connected by a steep flight of steps to a tunnel about 160 feet long, which led to a spring in an underground cave. Like the Siloam tunnel, it was cut by men working from opposite ends. The astounding skill of their technique and the accuracy of their calculations are shown by the fact that both in level and direction, the workmen were only two or three feet out of line when eventually they met in the middle. This centre point may be seen in the bend on the photograph(62), where it is marked by a metre stick. Although the credit for this hydraulic installation must be given to Canaanite engineers, it is of interest because it suggests that Israelite workmen learned the technique of boring tunnels from their predecessors in Palestine. Incidentally, it shows vividly how the Israelite women must have toiled at their water-carrying in later years, when they inherited the system and continued to use it.

There is one final significant example of engineering to record and that is the Great Shaft at Lachish. It is a curious rectangular excavation measuring $74 \times 84 \times 85$ feet, from which something like 500,000 cubic feet of solid limestone rock was quarried. It is not surprising that the leader of the party of excavators who tackled it in 1935 should have said that it was one of the greatest engineering feats achieved by the ancient craftsmen of Judah. It remains, however, an enigma; apparently, it was left unfinished and nobody is quite certain why it was started in the first place. It may have been the place from which stone was quarried to strengthen the walls of the city in an emergency, or it may have been intended as a water reservoir. Its exact date is no less difficult to determine, but it can be said with some assurance that it belongs to the century before the capture of the city in 586 B.C. A nice touch showing that these early engineers were as whimsical as they were tough is to be found on a projecting boulder near the bottom of the Great Shaft. In its natural state, it had reminded one of the workmen of a bearded man and so he was unable to forego the pleasure of adding a few finishing touches to make sure that the likeness would not be missed. It thereby becomes one of the rare pieces of native Israelite art!

LABOURERS AND SLAVES

Our new knowledge of the extensive industrial exploits of Solomon inevitably raises the labour question. Who did the work in his mines? What substitute did he possess for all the machinery (bulldozers, lifts, lorries and so on) which make it possible nowadays to build a new factory town almost overnight?

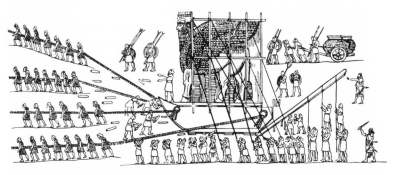

74   Gangs of Slaves moving an Assyrian monument

The ancient (and, indeed, the not-so-ancient) substitute for the machine was, of course, the slave. The Assyrian relief, showing gangs of men dragging an immense winged bull into position (74), graphically illustrates how the show-places of the ancient world were built by the toil and sweat of slaves.

Israel, we know, was no exception and Solomon's ambitious schemes could not have been carried through without the institution of State-slavery. Nelson Glueck, the distinguished American archaeologist, has discovered vast encampments for "Solomon's slaves" (as they came to be called) in and around the industrial centre of Ezion-geber. After they had built the town (73), no doubt they were employed on unskilled work at the foundries and smelteries. These wretched men, among whom the death-rate must have been enormously high, were obtained as prisoners of war from the Canaanites on the west of the Jordan and from Edom, Moab and Ammon, which Solomon conquered on the other side of the river.

The second and larger class of slaves, to whom most of the Old Testament laws refer, were privately owned. The State slaves were recruited almost exclusively from the ranks of prisoners of war; privately-owned slaves were predominantly Hebrews. The largest source of supply was the unhappy Israelite who found himself impoverished by war, bad harvests, bad lambing seasons and so on, and then by the exhorbitant rate of interest which was charged on the money he was forced to borrow to keep himself going. When he fell deeply into debt, his creditor was allowed by law to seize him and reduce him to slavery. For example, there is the pathetic incident of the

141

widow who came to the prophet Elisha, saying, "Thy servant my husband is dead: and thou knowest that thy servant did fear the Lord: and the creditor is come to take unto him my two children to be bondmen" (II Kings 4. 1). In this case, the father of the family had died, but often the children were actually sold by their parents. In addition to selling his children, a man was sometimes driven to sell himself as a slave, preferring the knowledge that the next meal was assured for his wife (who went with him) to the knowledge that they were both free—only to starve to death. It must often have happened that a debtor slave could not face the risks of setting up on his own again when his period of service was over. This situation is covered by an interesting law in Exodus 21. 2–6:

> If thou buy an Hebrew slave, six years he shall serve: and in the seventh he shall go out . . . by himself; if he be married, then his wife shall go out with him. If his master give him a wife, and she bear him sons or daughters; the wife and her children shall be her master's, and he shall go out by himself. But if the servant shall plainly say, I love my master, my wife, and my children; I will not go out free: then his master shall bring him unto God, and shall bring him to the door, or unto the door post; and his master shall bore his ear through with an awl; and he shall serve him for ever.

Nothing could better illustrate how a happy family life could be established in slavery and how a slave could come to love his owner, so that he refused to accept freedom after his six years' service. His solemn decision to enter into permanent slavery was witnessed by the domestic idols of the household (the "teraphim" discussed on p. 232), which probably lie behind the Hebrew word translated "God". It is difficult to make out whether this "permanent" slavery did, in fact, last for life. There is a late Old Testament law which enacts that even "permanent" slaves should be released every jubilee, that is, every fiftieth year. If this law was ever put into operation, it could have affected only a small number of slaves personally, but it would have ensured that a voluntary slave's grandchildren were free men and that no whole families were permanently reduced to slave status.

We should be making a big mistake, if we were to become theoretical about ancient Hebrew slavery and conclude that it was always miserable and degrading. It is true that from the stand-point of the law, a slave was a piece of property with a certain cash value. If, for example, a slave was killed by another man's goring ox, the owner of the ox had to pay the owner of the slave thirty shekels in compensation. This commercial transaction is in sharp contrast with the case of the goring of a freeman by an ox known to be dangerous. Then, its owner was guilty of murder and suffered the death penalty. Again, a master could beat his slave. If he died immediately, the master was liable to punishment, but if it could be established that the victim had lived for a day or two, the slave-owner got off scot-free, for (as the law put it succinctly), "he is his money".

Just as family relationships were not maintained at the low level of the law, so the relationship between master and slave often rose above it. Everything indeed depended on the character of the master and there is a good deal of evidence in the Old Testament to show that masters often treated their slaves with kindness and consideration. One of Abraham's slaves, for example, was not excluded from the possibility of becoming his heir (Genesis 15. 3); Abigail took her slave's advice (I Samuel 25. 14ff.); and Saul was obviously on terms of intimacy with his father's slave—even to the extent of borrowing money from him! These examples are confirmed by the generous treatment of slaves enjoined by many of the laws. For instance, the sabbath is explicitly described in Deuteronomy as an opportunity for slaves to take a rest and another law lays it down that at the end of his period of service, the freed slave should be well provided for: "And when thou lettest him go free from thee, thou shalt not let him go empty: thou shalt furnish him liberally out of thy flock, and out of thy threshing-floor, and out of thy winepress: as the Lord thy God hath blessed thee thou shalt give unto him" (15. 13f.).

In general, we may fairly say that both by instinct and religious conviction, the Israelites were opposed to slavery. The free life of the desert was not forgotten when the nomadic fathers settled down as farmers. The prophets' religious awareness of men's rights as *persons* is paralleled by the humanitarian intention of the laws and both reach their fitting climax in the book of Job, where it is explicitly asserted that slaves and freemen are equally creatures of God. By birth and before God, all men are equal. That is the conclusion of Old Testament religion and it is without parallel in the ancient Near East.

Chapter VII

MILITARY LIFE

THE Old Testament is notorious for its wars and rumours of wars and the casual reader might well be excused for thinking that in ancient Israel all everyday life was life in wartime. From the moment of the Exodus, we are nearly always within ear-shot of the trumpet and the din of battle. The wanderings in the wilderness are presented as a military campaign; the possession of Palestine was fought for fortress by fortress; and even after the Conquest, the Israelites engaged in almost incessant struggles with the vastly superior military powers on their borders. They never really found peace, until they lost their political independence with the fall of Jerusalem in 586 B.C.

The Israelites began their history with the belief that God would protect them as his Chosen People and fight their battles. If they had responded to the teaching of the prophets, they would have outgrown the cruder elements and dangers of this conception, but instead they adopted commercial and political ambitions which only served to strengthen them. Although the prophets protested against alliances based on armed strength and looked for the day when swords would be beaten into ploughshares, the men of Israel continued to delight in military prowess, which, they believed, God himself had taught them (Judges 3. 1f.). In consequence, their literature is dominated by the notion that war is holy, righteous and good.

The warrior inevitably enjoyed a high reputation in such a bellicose society and the very name for an aristocrat or leader of the community was borrowed from the "mighty men" of military valour.

MILITARY SERVICE

In the heroic days of Israel's early history portrayed in the book of Judges, there was no regular army, and the menfolk of the tribes fought their own battles. Military service was a religious obligation which all male adults (according to a late tradition those over the age of twenty) were expected to accept with enthusiasm. The savage vigour of Deborah's Song of Victory conveys much of the spirit of the volunteer in those days and illustrates the contempt and scorn poured on those who failed in their duty:

> Curse ye Meroz, said the angel of the Lord,
> Curse ye bitterly the inhabitants thereof;
> Because they came not to the help of the Lord,
> To the help of the Lord against the mighty (Judges 5. 23).

The founding of the monarchy and the establishment of a central government inevitably brought about big changes. Saul, we are told, collected all the valiant men he could find for his personal bodyguard (I Samuel 14. 52) and this corps formed the nucleus of a regular army. We do not know how far its organization was developed, but at least a permanent commander-in-chief was appointed. In his early days, David relied on a gang of semi-professional bandits and when he came to the throne, he greatly offended popular national sentiment by employing Philistines as mercenaries (II Samuel 15. 18). It was Solomon who really established a regular army and gave it the pattern which lasted nearly as long as the monarchy. The Old Testament historian is explicit: "And Solomon gathered together chariots and horsemen: and he had a thousand and four hundred chariots, and twelve thousand horsemen, which he bestowed in the chariot cities, and with the king at Jerusalem" (I Kings 10. 26). The excavations at Megiddo have confirmed the substantial truth of this statement (see pp. 66f.) and the discovery of the huge industrial plant at Ezion-geber (see p. 126) has gone a long way towards explaining how Solomon paid for so large and costly a military force. Whatever the exact arrangement of Solomon's High Command, there can be no doubt that it was extensive and included, at least, a senior officer in each of his fortified cities.

In times of grave emergency, the regular army was supplemented by an intake of national service men drawn from the cities. We hear of such city detachments incidentally from the prophet Amos (5. 3), and also in his time it is on record that the king employed a regular recruiting officer and a scribe who worked with him (II Chronicles 26. 11; compare II Kings 25. 19). The obligations of national service when the need arose are reflected in the very curious conscription law of Deuteronomy:

> And the officers shall speak unto the people, saying, What man is there that hath built a new house, and hath not dedicated it? let him go and return to his house, lest he die in the battle, and another man dedicate it. And what man is there that hath planted a vineyard, and hath not used the fruit thereof? let him go and return unto his house . . . And what man is there that hath betrothed a wife, and hath not taken her? let him go and return unto his house . . . And the officers shall speak further unto the people, and they shall say, What man is there that is fearful and fainthearted? let him go and return unto his house, lest his brethren's heart melt as his heart (20. 5–8).

It is difficult to think that a law with such sweeping exemptions was ever put into practice, but it does at least reinforce the idea that military service is too sacred to be undertaken by the half-hearted. Although the appearance of these provisions is humanitarian, they really spring from primitive religion, which gave rise to the belief that people who left a job unfinished were "unholy" and, therefore, a menace to the wellbeing of the rest of the armed forces.

It is probable that a "citizens' army" eventually replaced the professional army and that by the end of the seventh century B.C., the fortresses were manned by contingents of private citizens, who, even in peacetime, were called-up regularly for their period of military service.

ARMS AND EQUIPMENT

It is possible to describe the formidable war-machine of the Assyrians fairly precisely, as consisting of three arms—chariotry, cavalry and infantry; but the exact divisions and order of precedence in the Israelite army are much more elusive. It is fairly certain that the Hebrews had no cavalry until after the eighth century B.C. In 701 B.C., the offer of horses to the emissaries of Hezekiah appears to have been no more than a piece of mockery: "Now, therefore, I pray thee, give pledges to my master the king of Assyria, and I will give thee two thousand horses, *if thou be able on thy part to set riders upon them*" (II Kings 18. 23). In this respect, the Israelites were like the Egyptians, to whom also cavalry was unknown. The frequent references in the Old Testament to "horsemen" (e.g. II Kings 13. 7) are best understood as being due to an ambiguity of the Hebrew language and as referring properly to horses used in chariots.

Nor did the Israelite army possess any artillery, if we exclude the archers who fought from siege-engines. An isolated reference in II Chronicles ascribes the invention of a catapult to the reign of Uzziah in the eighth century B.C.: "And he made in Jerusalem engines, invented by cunning men, to be on the towers and upon the battlements, to shoot arrows and great stones withal" (26. 15); there is, however, no other evidence that the Israelites mounted catapults in this period, to which, in all probability, the Chronicler was reflecting back later developments.

As we should expect, the backbone of the army was the infantry. They alone could fight effectively in the mountains and no doubt it was they who persuaded the Syrians that the God of Israel was "a god of the hills" (I Kings 20. 23). Needless to say, the infantryman wore no uniform in our modern sense, and it is difficult to be sure how far the Hebrew armour of which we have information was used by the men as well as their officers. The enthusiastic Chronicler has it that Uzziah equipped all his troops with helmets and coats-of-mail (II Chronicles 26. 14). The officer's *helmet* (as worn by David and Goliath) was made of bronze, which remained popular for personal armour long after the introduction of iron. If the Assyrian fashion was followed in Israel, the helmet was high and pointed, with ear-pieces like an air-pilot's cap(75). The crest-mount and ear-piece of an Assyrian helmet, with scraps of leather and cloth still sticking to them, have been unearthed at Lachish. Bronze and iron scales from coats-of-mail have also been discovered there. The *coat-of-mail* was a heavy garment, consisting of a cloth or leather tunic to which metal scales were riveted in over-lapping formation; it may have been knee-length, but it was probably shorter. *Greaves* of bronze were worn on the legs, but leather *sandals* (see Isaiah 5. 27), rather than the high-laced boots of the Assyrians, appear to have been the only footwear. The infantryman's principal *weapons of attack* were sword, spear and lance. *Swords* were of different kinds, long and short, single- and double-edged, and sometimes so small that the distinction between sword and knife disappears;

147

in fact, the army private probably used his knife as an all-purpose implement—at home, in the vineyard, and on the battle-field. A well-preserved iron sword, about two feet long, single-edged and slightly curved, with rivets for attachment to its handle, has been discovered in a cistern at Debir, where it had lain since about 600 B.C. All swords were carried (probably sheathed) in a belt at the left side (unless, of course, a man was left-handed, like Ehud in Judges 3. 16).

The *spear* consisted of a bronze or iron head riveted to a wooden shaft and was primarily used for flinging at the enemy (as in I Samuel 18. 11). The *lance*, on the other hand, was lighter and shorter and was used as the chief weapon in hand-to-hand fighting.

75 Slingers of the Assyrian army

Slings were another important offensive weapon (75). To do them justice, we must forget the schoolboy's catapult and young David's shepherd sling, with its ammunition of smooth stones picked up from the river-bed (I Samuel 17. 40). Military slings were a serious weapon, whether we think of their being used by the seven hundred left-handed slingers of the tribe of Benjamin (Judges 20. 16), or by the warriors who made the king of Moab panic into sacrificing his son (II Kings 3. 25–27). The extensive use of the weapon is confirmed by the great number of flint balls (two to three inches in diameter) which have been found on Palestinian sites, and the seriousness with which it was regarded is attested by the care shown by the makers in giving a "finish" to this ammunition. The sling itself was made of leather or cloth, fashioned into a pocket to which cords were attached. The sling stone was whirled round in this pocket and released when the slinger let go one of the cords.

Even more important than slings, however, were the *bows*

148

and arrows of the archers. Arrowheads (mostly of iron) have now been unearthed by the hundred, many of them bent and broken by their impact with masonry. Most of those discovered are flat and leaf-shaped, without barbs. The *bow* was made of wood and its strings of gut or hide. The Assyrian reliefs show archers operating from the cover of enormous shields(76), which sometimes curved over the soldier's head to make a kind of canopy(78). Such bulky contraptions required the services of a shield-bearer, although, as they were made of plaited osiers, their weight was not necessarily very great. It is just possible that the Hebrew term for a *large shield* refers to this Assyrian type; it is more likely, however, that it means a wood and leather shield of convex design which covered the whole body. The ordinary infantryman carried a *small shield*, like the one shown on one of the Megiddo ivories(80).

After the infantry, the most important division of the Israelite army was the chariotry. In modern terms, the ancient *chariot* stands half-way between the armoured car and the jeep. It was used not so much for its weight as for its speed, being essentially a conveyance for the archer. For obvious reasons, it was suited to warfare in flat country, but was more or less useless in the mountains. This distinction explains why it was said that during the conquest of Palestine, God "drave out the inhabitants of the hill country; for he could not drive out the inhabitants of the valley, because they had chariots of iron" (Judges 1. 19). The Canaanites had used chariots long before the Israelite conquest (see p. 127), but the nomadic invaders knew so little of their value that they simply burnt them when they fell into their hands (Joshua 11. 6–9). It was Solomon who appreciated their worth, when he "mechanized" his army and

76   Archers with their Shield-bearer

149

established a great chariot force, which he garrisoned in strategic cities. After the division of the kingdom, Judah appears to have lost interest in chariots, but the northern kings still maintained a considerable number. An Assyrian inscription records that in the middle of the ninth century King Ahab of Israel had no less than 2,000 chariots and 10,000 infantry, thus giving us one of the more reliable figures for the size of the Israelite army in this period.

For information about the construction and appearance of the Israelite chariot, we have to rely on Egyptian and Assyrian illustrations, from which, however, we can draw a sufficiently accurate picture. When the Hebrew writers refer to "chariots of iron", they mean that they were plated or strengthened with iron; the main structure could be burnt and was undoubtedly made of wood. The "car" of the chariot was big enough to hold two or three men—the driver, the bowman and a shield-bearer to protect them. In the royal chariot(77), instead of the bowman, the crew included a personal attendant for the king, who either held his umbrella (as in the Assyrian reliefs) or steadied him as the chariot jolted over rough ground. The ancient method of "springing" a chariot was to make the floor of the car of some woven material (like rope or leather thongs); otherwise, vibration was reduced a little by setting the wheels as far back as possible. Nevertheless, the going must have been exceedingly rough. The wheels were large (from three to five feet in diameter) and their "tyres", which had iron plates or studs, were sometimes as much as ten inches thick. A curious artistic convention, which the Assyrians followed, assumes that the spectator is looking directly at the object and so seeing it in perfect profile; thus, it appears that chariots were drawn by a single horse, whereas, in fact, most of them had two horses in harness and often a third running free alongside as a spare. As the horse-collar had not yet been invented, at the end of the central shaft of the chariot, there was a yoke and it was to this that the driving-reins were attached. Sometimes, there appears to have been a third rein from the horses' bit to the front of the chariot and it is suggested that this was used for sudden braking. Protective cover for the animals was exceptional until about the seventh century B.C. The rest of the equipment of the chariot was simple. There were (? leather) holders (like golf bags) for bows, arrows and lances, which were usually placed

77   The Royal Chariot

on the right side of the vehicle, where the archer took his stand
(80). Since there was no room for seats, all the occupants stood.
The back of the chariot was usually left open, although in later
models it appears to have been protected by a fixed shield.

If chariots may be regarded as the armoured cars of Old
Testament times, the *battering-rams* were the tanks(78).
Perhaps, even, bulldozers would be a better analogy. The
prophet Ezekiel knew how they were employed in attacking a
city (4. 2) and it is probable that his countrymen used them
in their own offensive warfare. These ungainly engines are
very much in the forefront of the Assyrian reliefs and we can
well imagine how the Israelites dreaded the very sight of them.
The basic design looked rather like some prehistoric animal
and consisted essentially of a wooden framework mounted on
four or six wheels and covered with hide fastened down with
loops and pegs. Inside this framework a heavy wooden beam
was suspended by chains; its front end was weighted with
metal and gave the appearance of an animal's snout or the
pointed head of a ram. A crew of soldiers (how many we can
only guess) worked inside the engine and rocked the beam so
that it gathered enough momentum to shatter the masonry of
the enemy's fortifications.

Another variety of siege-engine familiar from the Assyrian

151

reliefs resembles an armoured truck with a hood-like shield raised high at the front. From behind this shield, archers fired into the enemy's defences on the top of the walls, while another member of the crew prodded the parapets with spear or pole. Perhaps this is the meaning of Ezekiel 26. 9: "his battering rams he places against thy walls and thy towers he demolishes with his lances". One amusing relief shows how the defenders tried to put such a machine out of action by hoisting up its pole on a loop of chain, while two soldiers of the attacking force struggled desperately to hold it down with grappling-hooks. Otherwise, these engines were attacked with blazing torches hurled from the walls of the city. The hide covering was easily set ablaze and evidently one member of the crew was detailed to act as fire-fighter. In one of the reliefs, a soldier may be seen using a long ladle for this purpose, but where he kept his water-supply is not shown, and it is difficult to imagine what he did about it. The acrid smoke of smouldering leather, combined with the laborious job of moving the engine and driving home the ram, must have made the manning of these primitive tanks one of the grimmest assignments in the army.

Any intelligent soldier would have tried to get a posting either to the Signals or the Service Corps. To speak of either as an independent unit in this period is no doubt an exaggeration, but the duties associated with these corps were certainly known in the army of Israel. For example, the end of the fourth of the Lachish Letters (see p. 183) reads: "We are looking for the signals of Lachish according to all the signs which my lord has given, for we do not see Azekah" (compare Jeremiah 34. 6f.). Presumably, these signals were fire signals (see Jeremiah 6. 1), and were a forerunner of wireless telegraphy as a means of communicating between fortified cities in time of war. Of the Service Corps, there is only one hint in the Old Testament. A special group (amounting to a tenth of the force) is detailed in Judges 20. 9f. to collect food for the rest of the army. Generally speaking, a soldier was kept supplied with food parcels from home (usually containing things like parched corn, dried raisins, bread and cheese) and when a campaign took him further afield, he had to rely on what he could scrounge in the countryside or pillage from the enemy. Again, it would be an exaggeration to speak of an Israelite Army Intelligence Corps or Secret Service, but the despatch of an advance party of spies

152

before an army took the field was regular military practice. Their methods and adventures are graphically depicted in the spy-story of Joshua 2. The work of the Engineers, a most important body of men, belongs to the details of siege-warfare, which will be considered below.

Of the Women's Services in our modern armies, only the redoubtable Deborah gives any anticipation!

FORTIFICATIONS

Cities in Old Testament times were built as fortresses and were enclosed within massive walls. Mizpah, a fairly small provincial city of Judah, was surrounded by a wall about 35 feet high and between 15 and 20 feet thick, set on a foundation of huge boulders with gaps between them—left, presumably, for drainage(17). The wall itself was built of limestone rocks set in clay mortar. Additional strength was afforded by buttresses at the bottom and by a number of rectangular towers built into the wall itself. The bases of these towers projected a couple of yards or so and were heavily fortified against attack by battering-rams and the mining operations of enemy sappers. In addition, the outer surface of the wall was coated with a thick layer of smooth plaster to a height of about 15 feet, apparently with the object of making it difficult to scale. Some cities were protected by a double wall. For example, Lachish (15) had an inner wall of brick about 20 feet thick, following the natural line of the escarpment and some 16 yards further down the slope of the mound, there was an outer wall made of stone. Both walls had a series of built-in towers.

Some city walls were built on the casemate principle, that is to say, there were really *two* walls, with thin inner partitions across the gap, forming small chambers between them. Some of these chambers were packed with rubble; others were supplied with doors on the city side and used as store-rooms. For example, Saul's citadel 3 miles north of Jerusalem had casemate fortifications, of which the outer wall was about 5 feet thick and the inner wall 4 feet. This method of building was borrowed from Syria and its great advantage was economy—in building materials, in labour and in space.

The weak spot in the city's defences and, therefore, the one most heavily fortified was the gate. The Israelites soon learnt that sheer weight of masonry was not enough and so they resorted to architectural guile. Instead of simply building the gate in the perimeter of the walls, they devised fairly elaborate gate plans which forced the invader to make an *indirect* approach to the city and to remain within the target area of the defending bowmen for the longest possible time. At Megiddo, the enemy was caught in a trap at the north gate(18) and so too at Lachish (15), where the gate fortifications formed a corridor between the inner and outer walls. The road running up to the gate at Lachish kept the right side of the enemy troops exposed for a long time to the fire of the archers stationed on the walls and the left turn demanded by the plan of the gate at Mizpah(19) must have considerably harassed attackers.

As time went on, it is clear that more attention was given to the building of special defence towers, both as part of the walls and detached from them. Their castellated design was evidently intended to give more scope to the bowmen of the defence force, who, from these vantage-points, could cover a considerable sector of the surrounding area. During a siege, it was sometimes the practice to build wooden galleries, projecting over the outer edge of the walls, in order to give the defenders a better chance of dropping missiles on the heads of the enemy.

WARFARE

Since the wars of Israel were believed to be the wars of Israel's God, the preparation for a campaign was religious as well as military. The armed forces were required to accept a specifically religious discipline, involving various kinds of abstention, to safeguard not so much their physical well-being as (that curious thing) the "holiness" of their undertaking. The campaign itself was inaugurated by a solemn act of sacrifice (I Kings 8. 44f.). The public intercessions made on such an occasion may be sampled in Psalm 20, which is a liturgical prayer (to accompany the sacrifice) for an Israelite king before he went to battle. The precise moment and circumstances for starting a campaign were determined (at least in theory) by consulting either professional prophets, as in the remarkable story of I Kings 22, or the sacred oracle in one or other of its many forms (see p. 221). By this means, it was believed, the will of God would be discovered. Such consultations were repeated at critical junctures in the campaign, and so no army was complete without priests who made divination their professional business.

Meanwhile, during the "cold" war, negotiations with the enemy would be conducted by special messengers (I Kings 20. 2–11), and only when their talks had broken down did the "hot" or "shooting" war begin. The troops were called to the colours by the blowing of trumpets throughout the land. Despite the deference shown to the will of God, it is unlikely that religious considerations were often allowed (either in Israel or among her neighbours) to conflict with military prudence and this demanded that campaigns should be undertaken only in the spring of the year, when food became available again after the winter shortage. This explains the phrase "at the return of the year, at the time when the kings march forth" (II Samuel 11. 1).

We have no means of rediscovering the technical details of Israelite military tactics. In the early days, when there was no standing army and no chariots or iron equipment for their troops, the Hebrews excelled only in surprise raids in difficult country. It is not long, however, before we hear of their fighters being drawn up in line and grouped in three separate divisions to launch their attack at three points simultaneously. The reorganization of the army under Solomon was clearly accompanied by developments in military tactics and (from Egyptian evidence) we may guess that archers usually opened the attack and were followed in due order by the chariotry and heavy infantry. It is at least certain that kings like Omri and Ahab were able generals and that their reputation spread through the whole of Syria. Another point about which there is no doubt is the practice of a "scorched-earth" policy. Elisha's instructions to his forces could not possibly be clearer: "And ye shall smite every fenced city, and every choice city, and shall fell every good tree, and stop all fountains of water, and mar every good piece of land with stones" (II Kings 3. 19). An attempt was made to control this wild savagery towards the end of the period and it finds expression in a law of Deuteronomy: "When thou shalt besiege a city a long time . . . thou shalt not destroy the trees thereof" (20. 19).

This law makes it clear that the Israelites used the technique of siege-warfare, which (according to II Samuel 20. 15) was practised as early as the reign of David. We do not know, however, to what extent the Israelite army was equipped with the battering-rams and the siege-engines, which appear on the Assyrian reliefs. It would be surprising, however, if Israel's military leaders had entirely failed to profit by their enemy's methods, even though their equipment was less streamlined than his. What is beyond doubt, as the same reliefs prove, is that the Israelites were the victims of full-scale siege-warfare(78).

The purpose of a siege was to isolate a city and compel its surrender by assault. When Sennacherib, the Assyrian, invaded Palestine in 701 B.C., he boasted that he shut up King Hezekiah "like a caged bird". The annals of his campaign, to be found on the Taylor Prism in the British Museum, contain this interesting passage:

> As for Hezekiah, the Jew, who did not submit to my yoke, 46 of his strong, walled cities, as well as the small cities in their neighbourhood, which were without number,—by escalade and by bringing up siege engines, by attacking and storming on foot, by mines, tunnels and breaches, I besieged and took. 200,150 people, great and small, male and female, horses, mules, asses, camels, cattle and sheep, without number, I brought away from them and counted as spoil. Himself, like a caged bird, I shut up in Jerusalem, his royal city. Earthworks I threw up against him. . . .[1]

One of the first objectives of the attacking force was the water-supply, for if this could be seized, the city was crippled. That is why the Israelites made such ingenious and elaborate attempts to construct waterworks inside their city walls (see pp. 137–40). As soon as the city was surrounded by the enemy's chariots and infantry, it was cut off from its main food-supply in the fields and vineyards of the "suburbs", and the besieged had to fall back on their stores of grain. When a siege lasted for months or (as sometimes happened) for years, these reserves soon ran low and rationing systems had to be introduced (Ezekiel 4. 10f.). Inevitably, the price of food soared on the blackmarket: "And there was a great famine in Samaria: and, behold, they besieged it, until an ass's head was sold for eighty silver shekels, and the fourth part of a kab [less than a pint] of dove's dung for five silver shekels" (II Kings 6. 25). Worse than bad food at fantastic prices and the disease which was bred by malnutrition, is the story of cannibalism with which

[1] The translation is taken from D. D. Luckenbill, *Ancient Records of Assyria and Babylonia.*

78   The Siege of a City

the historian continues his account of the plight of Samaria. It tells how two wretched women had agreed to eat their children and how one of them broke her bargain at the last moment. Many Old Testament references similarly illustrate the horrible straits to which the inhabitants of a besieged city were reduced (see, especially, Deuteronomy 28. 53–57).

Starving men will swallow anything and not least lying propaganda. It was left to the twentieth century to invent loudspeakers to blare accusations, fair promises and incitements to rebellion and desertion across the battlefront, but the Assyrians in Old Testament times were practising comparable psychological warfare on the Israelites. A splendid specimen of such a propaganda speech, addressed to the common people (and in their own language), may be found in II Kings 18. 17–37. The ghastly practice of impaling captives before the walls of a besieged city was another popular form of terrorism(8).

The major engineering operation in siege-warfare was the construction of a steep embankment against the city walls to enable the engines and battering-rams to be moved into position. This ramp was hastily thrown up with stones, soil and trees felled in the neighbourhood, the latter sometimes being used for laying a log track along which the machines could be dragged more easily. This must have been killing work (in every sense of the word) and, as we may safely guess, in carrying it out, "every head was made bald, and every shoulder was peeled" (Ezekiel 29. 18). Once in position, the battering-rams bashed the bottom of the wall in order to knock it down. From the more elaborate siege-engines, archers tried to establish supremacy of fire over the defenders, for the slingers and the bowmen on the walls were a considerable menace to the men exposed on the embankment. For this obvious reason, every attempt was made to dislodge the wooden parapets and galleries on top of the walls, from which the whole population of the city pelted the attackers with stones, arrows, blazing torches and anything they could lay their hands on. We are told in Judges 9. 53 that a "certain woman cast an upper millstone upon Abimelech's head, and brake his skull"; many kitchen utensils must have earned a comparable distinction.

There is abundant evidence that fire was one of the major dangers to be reckoned with on both sides during a siege.

Flaming torches were hurled on to the wooden engines and battering-rams and (as we have noticed) they had to be equipped with some kind of fire-fighting apparatus. In return, every effort was made to set fire to the city itself. The parapets, galleries and half-timbered buildings were highly combustible and soft limestone, we are told, offers little resistance to heat. The official report of the excavation of Lachish describes the devastation caused by fire when it was demolished by the Babylonian army just before the fall of Jerusalem:

> Masonry, consolidated into a chalky white mass streaked with red, had flowed in a liquid stream over the burnt road surface and lower wall, below which were piled charred heaps of burnt timber. In the angle below the north wall of the Bastion and the west revetment, breaches which had been hurriedly repaired with any material available were forced again; indeed, evidence of destruction by fire was not difficult to find anywhere within the circuit of the walls. Whether all the damage was done at the time of attack is uncertain. In the case of Jerusalem, the burning of the temple, the palace and the houses was the result of a systematic policy put into force by the troops a month after the capitulation, and the same method may have been used at Lachish.[1]

Fire was also used as a weapon by the sappers. Their main job was to undermine the walls of the city and one of their favourite methods was to dig a great hole at the base, shore up the masonry with timber (like pit-props), and then set fire to the wood so that the wall collapsed into the pit prepared for it. The defending sappers not only tried to repair breaches in the wall as best they could (and this sometimes meant quarrying limestone within the city boundaries), but also attempted to seize the enemy sappers and their earthworks by digging counter tunnels from the inside.

The climax of a siege, when the forces of the city were spent by casualties, disease, and utter weakness was the scaling of the walls with ladders. This was the final terror.

DEFEAT AND VICTORY

The treatment of a conquered city was a curious combination of religion, greed and cruelty. Ancient religious ideas, shared by Israel with her neighbours, demanded that the god of battle should receive his share of the spoils of victory. The motives

[1] Olga Tufnell, *Lachish III*, The Iron Age, p. 57.

underlying this conviction were, no doubt, extremely mixed and differently emphasized according to place and period. There seems, however, to have been fairly general agreement that objects of especial value belonged by right to the victorious deity and should be placed in his sanctuary. This explains why conquerors always found temple treasures so tempting. The offering of a proportion of the plunder to the sanctuary was no less ambiguous than other forms of sacrifice. On the one hand, the gift could be crudely regarded as the due reward for work well done, and as an encouragement to the god to give similar support in the future; and, on the other hand, its acceptance by the god was thought of as "neutralizing" the pollution which inevitably attached to enemy property and as making it safe for his people to take their share of it.

An extreme form of this sacrificial offering was the "ban", by which the fruits of victory were cut off from profane use and "devoted" to the god by complete destruction. In practice, this meant the wholesale slaughter of the enemy and the burning of his city to the ground. When Samuel hewed Agag in pieces, he was correcting Saul's unorthodox decision to spare him (I Samuel 15. 9, 32f.), and the wretched Achan was himself destroyed for sneaking a cloak and precious metals from Jericho after it had been "banned" and, therefore, scheduled for complete demolition (Joshua 7). Since religious theory is often more extreme than actual practice, it is impossible to be certain how far the Israelites carried out this appalling doctrine. The likelihood is that it remained in the background as a living idea, conveniently forgotten when the spoil was wanted, and invoked, as required, to disguise bitter enmity and plain cruelty.

The Old Testament does nothing to conceal the Israelites' liking for booty. The chief share, of course, went to the king and the rest was divided between the fighting men and the men at base. Most probably, this was the only source of a soldier's pay and was, therefore, vital to the morale of the troops. One of the most valuable forms of booty was prisoners for slave labour, which Solomon exploited for his extravagant enterprises (see p. 141).

Enslavement was by no means the worst of the horrors which threatened the victims of Assyrian conquest, even though it often meant a premature death in the swamps of Mesopotamia.

79 Assyrians bringing in enemy Heads and Prisoners to be recorded by the Scribes

Many were killed during the systematic sacking and burning of the captured city. At Lachish, for example, a tomb has been excavated which contained the scattered bones of about 1,500 people, of whom an unusually high proportion appear to have died relatively young. They had been thrown into the tomb higgledy-piggledy and covered with a layer of animal bones— mostly from pigs! It has been suggested that this jumbled mass represents the clearance of the city after the Assyrian siege of 701 B.C. and that the pig bones were left over from the kitchens of the enemy.

Many who were taken prisoner must have welcomed death. The Assyrian monarchs, ceremonially enthroned at the captured city gate, used to entertain themselves by arranging a ghastly human circus, in which the chief men of the community were brought on to the scene, either in cages or in chains, and then tortured, blinded or burnt alive. One Assyrian king boasted that he had erected a human column of writhing agony. Meanwhile, royal scribes counted the heads of the common people, before they were piled up in bloody pyramids(79). When eventually the doom of the Assyrian Empire was sealed and Nineveh, its capital, fell in 612 B.C., it is not surprising that the book of Nahum should have been written in a spirit of savage jubiliation.

The other side of this grim picture was the victorious home-coming. The column of warriors, smaller than when it set out,

161

was sighted from the city a great way off. The news spread like wild-fire from roof-top to roof-top and everybody downed tools. Within a matter of minutes, the narrow alleys were crammed with women and children, pushing and shoving to get to the gate. The months of the men's absence had been tiring and anxious, even more anxious than tiring, for though work in the fields was hard, the lot of the widow in Israel was harder. And now the haunting fear, which was never openly admitted, would soon be confirmed or dispelled. The children were already scrambling down the rough road of the rampart shrilling their welcome, and among the excited young women singing had started. There would be more singing in the evening and the next day, with much drinking of wine, receiving of presents, and telling of tales. Then the winter would come with the rains and the ploughing, and the trumpet remain silent until the spring of the year.

Chapter VIII

CIVIL LIFE

THE system of government under which the Israelites lived was completely revolutionized during Old Testament times. When the men of Judah were deported to Babylon at the end of the period, they were the subjects of an absolute monarch, whereas the only form of political organization known to their ancestors when they entered Palestine seven centuries earlier was that of the tribe.

It is fairly easy to follow the stages in the break-up of tribal life and the establishment of a powerful central government, but it is less easy to discover how this development affected the ordinary citizen. In what ways does any system of government influence the everyday life of an ordinary family living miles away from the capital? First of all, it may interfere with the freedom of its members. Secondly, by taxation, it may make a great difference to their standard of living. Thirdly, the maintenance of law and order depends upon good government and the local judicial system has a very direct bearing on everyday life. Finally, whether or not a government enters into commercial and political relations with other countries influences in the long run the humblest of its subjects. These four factors, which are, of course, intimately related, suggest topics for a sketch of Israel's civil life, but as they all depend on the status of the king, a brief description of his office must be given first.

THE KING

A comparison between the rustic court of Saul and the Oriental splendour with which Solomon surrounded himself demonstrates better than anything else how fully and how early Israel came to adopt the exalted and despotic notion of kingship current in the Near East.

Saul was ploughing in the fields when he was called to be king and he remained a farmer among his own people throughout his reign. When he sat down to dinner, four places were laid; when he held court, he sat under a tamarisk tree. Solomon, on the other hand, was born in the purple. He erected a splendid

163

80   His Majesty the King
(*see footnote*)

new palace and temple next to each other in his capital, since it was only fitting that God and his earthly representative should occupy adjacent houses. The coronation ceremony at which he was anointed and enthroned assured the sanctity of his person and set him apart from his fellow countrymen. His crown was really a form of the high-priestly "mitre" and it characterized his high office as being essentially religious. His magnificent throne of ivory and gold, its steps flanked by sculptured lions, was copied from the best foreign models; so, to a large extent, was the idea of its occupant's absolute authority(80).[1]

Solomon's entourage at court was immense and from the fact that they were called "those who saw the face of the king", we may gather that they screened their royal master from the gaze of the common people. Many of the offices of the royal household had been established in David's reign, but his son greatly increased their number. We hear of the "Makir" (literally, the "remembrancer") at the head of the political administration, the Secretary of State, the Keeper of the Palace, the Chancellor of the Exchequer, the Minister of (Forced) Labour, the King's Adjutant, the Keeper of the Wardrobe, not to speak of court priests, army officers and scores of minor flunkeys. The assertion that Solomon's harem consisted of 1,000 women should be taken with a pinch of salt, but we need not doubt that so important a piece of royal shop-window dressing was made very impressive. This vast organization, probably modelled on the high-powered bureaucracy of Egypt,

[1] This ivory from Megiddo (dated about 1200 B.C.) shows (on the left) a Canaanite king sitting on a throne flanked by winged lions with human heads. He drinks from a bowl, as one of his musicians entertains him on the lyre. On the right, a bearded driver (who may, possibly, be the king himself) stands in a chariot holding a whip. The chariot is drawn by two horses and equipped with two quivers and a lance. Before it, two nude prisoners are driven, their hands tied and fastened to the horses' harness. A warrior, armed with a pike and a small round shield, goes before them. The whole scene admirably illustrates Solomon's notion of kingship.

164

owed its authority and loyalty neither to People nor Parliament (the first did not matter and the second did not exist), but to the King alone.

CONSCRIPTION

The kind of impact which Israel's new type of government made on everyday life may be assessed, if we make due allowance for exaggeration, by the terms in which it was criticized by a later Old Testament writer who chose Samuel as his mouth-piece:

> This will be the manner of the king that shall reign over you: he will take your sons, and appoint them unto him, over his chariots, and over his horses; and they shall run before his chariots: and he will appoint them unto him for captains of thousands, and captains of fifties; and he will set some to plough his ground, and to reap his harvest, and to make his instruments of war, and the instruments of his chariots. And he will take your daughters to be perfumers, and to be cooks, and to be bakers. And he will take your fields, and your vineyards, and your oliveyards, even the best of them, and give them to his servants. And he will take the tenth of your seed, and of your vineyards, and give to his officers, and to his servants. And he will take your menservants, and your maidservants, and your goodliest young men, and your asses, and put them to his work. He will take the tenth of your flocks: and ye shall be his bondmen (I Samuel 8. 11–17).

Not every item in this catalogue of crimes can be substantiated from our records, but there is enough confirmation to suggest that the writer was not simply fabricating abuse.

Although Solomon established a regular army, it was augmented by conscripts in times of national emergency. The Israelites as a people were not averse to fighting, but they may well have resented the king's recruiting officer, and no doubt, many of the military expeditions for which he enlisted troops.

There is no other evidence outside the passage just quoted that the king abused his power to the extent of commandeering the services of Israelite women for work on the domestic staff of the palace, but there is nothing wildly improbable in the accusation. We know as a fact that he pressed 30,000 of his male subjects into labour gangs, which was a far bolder innovation. These Israelite conscripts were taken away from their farms and their families one month in every three to hew cedars in Lebanon. We may estimate the social upheaval which this caused in the country by the fact that it involved an estimated 4 per cent of the total population. It is not easy to imagine about 2,000,000 British citizens working four months of the year as labourers on Government building schemes, but an imposition of that order is what the independent-minded Israelites had to tolerate. At a later date, we are told, Asa issued a proclamation to Judah exacting conscript labour for further royal projects (I Kings 15. 22) and it is probable that the detested *corvée* was maintained as long as the monarchy survived. The wonder is that it survived at all.

TAXATION

Even those Israelites who were not sufficiently politically-minded to resent the growth of a highly centralized form of government soon began to resent the development when they found that they had to help pay for it. David had undoubtedly cherished ideas of introducing an efficient system of taxation, but it was left to his son to realize his intention.

Solomon divided the country into twelve administrative districts, in each of which he placed a Higher Civil Servant, whose duty it was to supply the court with provisions for one month a year. These tax districts cut across some of the old tribal divisions and their officers (of whom two significantly were Solomon's sons-in-law) were from Jerusalem and not local men. It was a case of "government from Whitehall". According to I Kings 4. 22, the needs of the court were anything but modest and included *daily* "thirty measures of fine flour, and sixty measures of meal; ten fat oxen, and twenty oxen out of the pastures, and an hundred sheep". If these figures are to be trusted, each administrative district had to supply an annual average of roughly 5,000 bushels of flour, 10,000 bushels of meal, 900 oxen and 3,000 sheep. Since the population of a district has been estimated at less than 100,000 persons, it is not surprising that the burden of taxation led to the rebellion which followed Solomon's death.

Solomon's division of the country for taxation survived him and probably lasted as long as the monarchy. At least, the so-called Samaritan Ostraca (see pp. 182f.) give us direct evidence from the time of Amos of an organized system of taxation in the Northern Kingdom. These small fragments of broken pottery, found in one of the storehouses of Jeroboam II's palace at

Samaria, had evidently been used as receipts for oil and wine. For example, one of them reads:

> In the tenth year.
> To Gaddiyau.
> From Azah.
> Abi-ba'al 2
> Ahaz 2
> Sheba 1
> Meriba'al 1

Apparently, Gaddiyau was the royal tax officer; Azah the district or village sending its payment of wine or oil and the other persons named farmers credited with a certain number of jars.

There is also archaeological evidence from the Southern Kingdom which probably shows a similar system of taxation in operation during the two centuries before the Exile. This consists of a collection of 550 handles from storage jars, found at no less than fourteen sites in Judah, bearing stamp impressions. One of the jars discovered at Lachish has been reconstructed(69) and found to have a capacity of ten gallons. On each of its four handles, there had been stamped a four-winged symbol representing an Egyptian flying beetle with an inscription written above and below, reading "lam-melekh Hebron". (The left-hand drawing in the illustration(81) gives a fair impression of the appearance of the stamp, although the Hebrew lettering is imperfect.) Some of the other jar stamps have a simpler two-winged symbol, which has been variously identified as the winged solar disc of Egypt, a flying scroll (like the one described in Zechariah 5), and a bird (see the right-hand sketch in the illustration(82); the right edge is properly the bottom edge of the seal impression). Instead of "lam-melekh Hebron", which means "to (or, of) the King—*Hebron*", other seals read "to the King—*Ziph*", or "to the King—*Sokoh*", or "to the King—*Memshath*", of which all but the last are identifiable place-names.

Scholars have found the interpretation of this material difficult, but there is weighty support for the view that the stamped jars were used for collecting taxes paid to the king in kind, principally wine and oil. The first part of the inscription "to the King" is generally agreed to be equivalent to our O.H.M.S. (On Her Majesty's Service), which still gives the

167

81, 82 Jar-handle Stamps: *left*, a four-winged beetle; *right*, a two-winged symbol

official stamp to demands for the payment of income tax. Its meaning may be more specific and refer to the officially-gauged capacity of the jar (see pp. 190 f.). The significance of the four names is still debated, but many experts think that they are the names of local tax centres, where the oil and wine were collected and stored before being sent to Jerusalem. It is fortunate that we can supplement in this way the very scanty Old Testament evidence of the cost to the ordinary farmer of an ambitious and extravagant government. The casual reference of Amos to "the king's mowings" (7. 1) suggests that the Crown also demanded the first cut of grass for its army horses. How much more taxation there was of a similar kind we are left to guess.

LAW AND ORDER

The power of traditional law, which ensured the order and well-being of the community, was one of the strongest forces in Israelite life. Every Hebrew boy was brought up in an atmosphere of legal discussion, not indeed the argumentation of professional lawyers, but the unending deliberations of the most respected members of the community, as they dispensed justice in conformity with recognized custom. In the tribal life of the desert, disregard of custom was too dangerous to be tolerated, and the consequent deep-rooted respect for law and order survived the change to an urban way of living. It also survived the development of the power of the monarchy. Although the king was *ex officio* Chief Justice, he himself was not above the law and however much he departed from the old ways in other directions, the elders, who were the guardians of ancient custom, held their own against him. Their authority was recognized even in the celebrated case of *Rex* v. *Naboth*, when even the king's wife knew that the only way of succeeding in her outrageous plot was to collaborate with the leading men of Naboth's family city (I Kings 21. 8 ff.). Outside the capital, where, presumably, the king's power reigned supreme through his personal officers, the maintenance of law and order remained in the hands of local Justices of the Peace. It is not easy to determine the relationship between these J.P.'s and the priest of the local sanctuary. In Israel, there was no sharp division between civil and "ecclesiastical" law and the likelihood is that only the difficult cases, in which the court of the elders could not reach a decision, were referred to the sanctuary officials.

In order to understand the working of Israel's judicial system, we must remember that there was no statutory law or code of detailed regulations, no police force and no Public Prosecutor. All the cases considered by the judges were brought by individuals with a grievance. The plaintiff and defendant appeared in person before the bench at the gate of the city (see p. 61) and brought with them their witnesses, any material evidence (like the remaining fragments of a worried sheep; see p. 50), and, no doubt, a large crowd of their friends and relations. There were always at least two witnesses and their responsibility was a heavy one. It must, indeed, have been a red-letter day in a young man's life when he made his maiden speech as a witness at the gate. If the evidence of the witnesses resulted in the death penalty, they were the men to cast the first stone; if they were found guilty of false witness, they themselves were sentenced to the punishment which fitted the alleged crime. If the nature of the case excluded the possibility of witnesses (e.g. an action concerning the theft of an animal), the accused person had to vindicate himself by oath before the priests at the sanctuary. This practice probably explains why the Book of Psalms contains so many prayers in which an accused man protests his innocence (see, for example, Psalms 5, 7, 17 and 26). Such pieces may well represent, or derive from, standard oaths of purgation. How the priests arrived at their verdict we do not know. They may have used some form of ritual divination (see p. 221) or trial by ordeal, of which there is an isolated example in Numbers 5. 11–31; but whatever their means, the result was held to be the binding verdict of God himself.

The court never imposed fines or committed a man to prison. For the less serious offences, the guilty person was sentenced to be beaten with a rod up to a maximum of forty stripes and the punishment was administered there and then in the presence of the judges. Small wonder that there was never a dull moment at the gate of an Old Testament city! For capital offences (to us a curious collection ranging from murder to a son's rebellion

169

83 International goods

against his parents), the punishment was stoning, which was executed outside the city wall. By a barbarous custom, the whole population joined in and pelted their victim until he was completely buried. In especially infamous cases, the corpse was subsequently burned, or impaled and left hanging for a period.

A curious fact about the specification of these punishments in the Old Testament is the absence of any suggestion that the convicted person was in disgrace. It is almost beyond our comprehension that the law should solemnly limit the beating of a convicted criminal to forty stripes in order to safeguard his personal *honour* (Deuteronomy 25. 3). Nothing could better remind us how hard it is for the modern West to understand the ancient East.

COMMERCE

The reputation of the Jews as good business people did not begin until after the Exile and then they went into commerce more by necessity than desire. In Old Testament times, relatively few private citizens became important merchants and the reason is not difficult to discover. In a land which was predominantly agricultural, most people grew their own food and the peasant farmers could ill-afford the luxury of what our modern jargon calls "consumer goods". In any case, the

170

traffic by Camel

importation of luxuries was beset by transport difficulties. When, nowadays, the smallest trader can offer his customers in the remotest village food-stuffs in fresh condition from every part of the world, it is difficult to remember that the Israelites depended for transport almost exclusively on camels(83). Asses were of very limited value for the long treks demanded by international trade and the complete absence of metalled roads held up any development towards improving wheeled vehicles. The use of horses was confined to drawing chariots and only kings employed chariots for any but military purposes. Even then (as we may gather from I Kings 18. 44), a shower of rain was enough to make the royal chariot driver hurry home before he got bogged. The carts to which the Old Testament makes reference were little more than farm carts, drawn by oxen and capable of carrying only comparatively small loads(84). It is not surprising, therefore, that the commerce of Palestine was beyond the capacity of the ordinary individual and became the virtual monopoly of kings. Their only effective competitors were the semi-nomadic peoples who spent their lives plying the great international trade-routes between Egypt, Arabia, Syria and Mesopotamia with their long camel trains (see map on p. 43) and even these were compelled to pay toll into the royal coffers as they passed through Israelite territory.

171

When Solomon came to the throne, circumstances were unusually favourable for the development of commerce on the grand scale. Israel's boundaries had been extended and her control of the caravan routes secured by David; the sea power of Phoenicia had revived after an unsettled period and the Mediterranean was under her control; and, finally, the camel (only recently domesticated) was opening up new possibilities of trade with Arabia.

Solomon seized his opportunities with both hands. His most original adventure was a trading agreement with Phoenicia. By this arrangement, he not only secured skilled architects and craftsmen for his building schemes, but was able to establish a merchant fleet on the Red Sea. Very few of his land-locked subjects had so much as seen a ship, and so the building of Israel's vessels was entrusted to Phoenician experts. Their design was probably somewhere between that of the early battleship(85) and the later trading vessel(6). The most striking feature of the battleship is the pointed ram in front for attacking enemy vessels. The oarsmen, it will be noticed, were arranged in two rows on the lower deck; the upper deck was occupied by soldiers and passengers and protected by a line of shields. Two large oars served as rudders and the sail (on a single yard) was of a type which is easily furled. Solomon's naval base was Ezion-geber, which he developed into one of the most advanced industrial centres of the ancient world. His merchant fleet took cargoes of copper ingots to Ophir, a district which has not been identified with certainty, but which probably means the south-west of Arabia and possibly parts of the

84 A typical Israelite Cart. The Assyrians are taking it as part of their spoil from the city of Lachish. Notice the dress of the women in 701 B.C.

85   A Phoenician Battleship

African coast opposite. Its design and merchandise explain why it was called a "navy of Tarshish" (*tarshish* meaning a refinery), like other fleets engaged in similar traffic in the Mediterranean. The round-trip from Ezion-geber to Ophir and back took three years and when the fleet returned to base it brought, we are told, "gold, and silver, ivory, and apes, and peacocks" (I Kings 10. 22), as well as sandalwood and precious stones. Unlike modern governments, Solomon did not have to consider public opinion or popular demand when he allocated his shipping space to the various commodities. Most of them found their way to Jerusalem. This new Israelite maritime venture clearly challenged the overland caravan trade with Arabia and it has been plausibly suggested that when the Queen of Sheba paid her famous visit to Solomon (so superbly reported in I Kings 10), she had it in mind, not only to profit by the king's wisdom, but also to tempt him into a trading agreement. If the story is reliable, she got what she wanted.

Ezion-geber remained an important centre of the Arabian trade after Solomon's death, but we do not hear of the fleet after the middle of the ninth century B.C., when, we are told laconically, "Jehoshaphat made ships of Tarshish to go to Ophir for gold: but they went not; for the ships were broken at Ezion-geber" (I Kings 22. 48). With that storm, Israel's seafaring days came to an end.

Hardly less remarkable than his Red Sea venture, was

173

Solomon's monopoly of the trade in horses and chariots. Our information about it is given in a difficult passage, which Professor Albright has translated as follows:

> And Solomon's horses were exported from Cilicia: the merchants of the king procured them from Cilicia at the current price; and a chariot was exported from Egypt at the rate of six hundred shekels of silver and a horse from Cilicia at the rate of a hundred and fifty; and thus (at this rate) they delivered them by their agency to all the kings of the Hittites and the kings of Aram (I Kings 10. 28 f).[1]

It is clear that the king and his agents were the middle-men between Syria (supplying horses) and Egypt (supplying chariots) and that the rate of exchange was four horses to one chariot. We have no means of discovering what percentage Solomon exacted as commission, but the arrangement has every appearance of having been a piece of profitable business.

As wealth poured into Israel, not only during Solomon's reign, but later under Omri and Ahab in the ninth century B.C. and Jeroboam II and Uzziah in the eighth century B.C., what was happening among ordinary people, to whom gold and ivory, apes and peacocks were no more than a fabulous dream? A large part of the answer to this question has already been suggested in our sketch of Israel's history (pp. 34–7). There is no doubt that the royal trading monopoly stimulated private enterprise. The kings had imported into Israel not only tempting luxury goods on which to spend money, but an even more seductive new standard of values, which encouraged the worship of the Almighty Shekel. The small army of civil servants distributed throughout the length and breadth of the land on the king's business helped point the way to what, had the words been coined, would have been called Prosperity and Progress. Their residences, their furniture, their modern sanitation and their manner of life showed what money could buy. These things disturbed the peace of rural Palestine; new classes and class-divisions came into being and the old easy-going democratic tradition of Israel was snuffed out.

By the very nature of things, only the improved material amenities of the *nouveaux riches* have survived the centuries for the spade of the excavator. The haunting fears and empty

---

[1] *Archaeology and the Religion of Israel*, p. 135.

stomachs of the peasant leave no memorial, unless (as happened in Israel) they attract the sympathetic attention of a more articulate section of society. Prophets like Amos, Isaiah and Micah were nothing if not articulate. They tell us in no uncertain terms what commercial progress meant in everyday life—vulgar ostentation, licentiousness, land-grabbing, swindling in the markets and corruption in the courts. It was Isaiah (and not a nineteenth-century social reformer) who first spoke of "grinding the face of the poor". The prophets' report of what was going on behind the prosperous veneer of gold and ivory is confirmed by many details in the law book Deuteronomy, which belongs to the last years of our period. By this time, it was necessary to legislate for false weights and measures, debt, usury, slavery, the treatment of hired labourers, and the alleviation of the lot of the poor. So much for the wisdom of Solomon.

The commercial expansion of Israel was, however, only one part of a wider national ambition—that of playing an imperial role in Near Eastern politics. It was a silly and disastrous game. Israel's native resources were inadequate to sustain a position of leadership, and her dependent alliances with the great Powers brought her nothing but financial ruin and, finally, political annihilation. Those who cared for the moral and spiritual well-being of the people were not slow to point out that you couldn't import the wealth of the nations without their debased religion. Trafficking in foreign gods undermined the very foundation of the nation's life.

Chapter IX

PROFESSIONAL LIFE

IT is instructive to discover that the manifold activities of Israel's everyday life refuse to group themselves in the neatly-labelled categories which we take for granted. Consider, for example, education, popular science, medicine, music and art, which form the subject of the present chapter. In the twentieth century, they would all be regarded broadly as "cultural" pursuits, but this description hardly fits the type of education given to a largely illiterate population, the kind of medicine which drew more on primitive superstitions than on scientific observation, or a form of art of which the style was largely borrowed and the execution more or less restricted to the craftsman who worked in ivory and precious stones. This term "cultural", with its inevitable suggestion of refinement and sophistication, undoubtedly will not serve.

A tempting alternative label is "intellectual", which from our point of view would be justified by the fact that you can read all these subjects (except *popular* science!) even in the most conservative of our ancient universities. But again, the question arises, in what sense may the evocative and un-systematized music of the Hebrews (not to speak of the other subjects) be truly described as engaging the intellect? This question immediately prompts another of wider scope: in what sense may the Hebrews be said to have had any intellectual interests at all? The subject deserves careful analysis in a large volume; here, a brief digression must suffice.

The Old Testament does not contain a single word of analytical or speculative philosophy; it is innocent of logic and never argues. Although its overwhelming concern is with God, since it never doubts or abstractly considers his existence, it offers no proofs for it. It shows no inhibitions about the use and abuse of language, but employs words with spontaneity and abandon. They pile up in rich confusion, concrete and colourful. Metaphors abound and most of them are splendidly mixed. From all this verbal energy, no definitions emerge of the kind which enables you to say with precision what something is *not*, but there does emerge a persuasive communication of what that something is at its centre. A poet does not define; he conveys the character of a scene or a situation as it affects *him*. In this sense, the Hebrews were poets. Their language did not permit them any different kind of precision. It is weak in all the tools which delight the heart of philosopher and pedant—technical terms, abstract nouns, and card-indexed adjectives. It is strong, on the other hand, in all that everyday life demands of a language—verbs and again verbs—to express doing and feeling. If language be admitted as evidence, the Greeks' 100,000 words to 1,800 verbal roots reveals a much more intellectual approach to life than that of the Hebrews, who possessed a mere 10,000 words for their 2,000 roots. In the Old Testament, you can never escape people busily *doing* things, nor the deep conviction that people matter more than anything but God. Its writers never become airborne with ideas; they look up to heaven, but their feet are flat on the earth.

Between heaven and earth, however, they appreciated both a likeness and a difference and this awareness was intellectual in the sense in which all religion transcends the immediate world of ordinary experience. The similarity and contrast between God and man was not, however, explored and analysed by the Hebrews. Occasionally it was stated in simple terms, but more often it was implied in their magnificent capacity for the making and breaking of verbal images. The Old Testament writers draw on the whole of everyday life in their attempts to convey the character of God in metaphors, but they are never so naïve as to suppose that they have described or defined his nature. Before a metaphor has a chance of becoming an intellectual substitute for God, it is broken by the onrush of another image, which in its turn is discarded as soon as it has served its purpose. The Israelites no more tolerated idols of the mind and the imagination than idols of silver and gold. Their iconoclasm has much to teach those who purvey popular science and popular Christian doctrine in the twentieth century.

If we conclude that "cultural" and "intellectual" are misleading labels for the subjects of this chapter, we must fall back on the loose term "professional". We may legitimately do so, not only because in Old Testament times there were professional musicians, professional scribes and a handful of professional artists, in the sense of their being full-time specialists, but also because their work was recognized as being intrinsically important quite apart from its financial reward, which is perhaps the definitive feature of any profession.

EDUCATION

The Israelites were in no sense a "bookish" people and it is obvious that their literary culture was greatly inferior to that of the Canaanites, the Egyptians and the Babylonians.

The average boy of (say) Isaiah's time never went to school; in fact, the Old Testament has no word for school and professional teachers are not referred to explicitly until a much later period. What he learnt he would get in the first place from his mother and then, as he grew up, his father took over the responsibility for his training. His sister's education was entirely in her mother's hands. There is a little evidence to show that the boys of wealthy parents were brought up by guardians (which is no more than we should have guessed), but such special tutors must have been quite exceptional.

As there was nothing like a State educational system, children were taught the essentials at home. For the girls, the training was concerned almost exclusively with becoming a good wife and mother, whereas the boys were taught to follow in their father's footsteps. The book of Proverbs frequently emphasizes the importance of religious and moral instruction and this too was given by the parents at home. It would be mistaken to assume that such instruction came only or mainly from books. Eastern peoples have always relied a good deal on oral tradition and the Old Testament itself is a collection of literature which was meant to be read *aloud*. It is extremely probable that a great deal of it was originally handed down by word of mouth in a way which the man of the West (with his daily newspapers, reference libraries and weak capacity for remembering) can hardly expect to understand fully. We are to imagine, therefore, the father of the family and sometimes a professional story-teller recounting the great stories of Israel's national heroes to an audience gathered on the roof-top or at the gate of the city. On many such occasions, religious instruction and sheer entertainment must have been very difficult to disentangle the one from the other.

It is impossible to say what proportion of the population were taught to read and write, but the likelihood is that it was

178

very small indeed. It is true that Isaiah distinguishes between the literate and illiterate (29. 12) and mentions in one passage (10. 19) a child's writing, but he was in close touch with the aristocratic circle of the court and capital and his casual references cannot be used as the basis for a sweeping generalization. Far more significant of the general state of affairs is the revealing fact that when an Israelite borrowed money, he did not write a chit (like an I.O.U.), but gave a garment in pledge. The garment had no security value and was probably used as a symbol of indebtedness by the illiterate.

On the other hand, it is quite certain that *some* boys were taught to read and write, and it is even possible that we still possess evidence of their writing exercises. The rough scribbling which is now known as the Gezer Calendar (see p. 98) has been plausibly interpreted as a student's effort and in 1938 somebody spotted the first five letters of the Hebrew alphabet scratched *in their conventional order* on the vertical face of a step of the royal palace at Lachish. Experts date this inscription in the early part of the eighth century B.C. and they have suggested that it was written by a boy who was just learning his ABC. If, indeed, the alphabet was being systematically taught at this period (and that is what the inscription suggests), there must have been more formal instruction than we know of otherwise. Probably, it was the work of the scribes. It is even possible to eavesdrop on a children's spelling lesson in a passage of Isaiah, where the prophet is being mocked by a group of men who say that he treats them like infants:

> Whom will he teach knowledge?
>> whom will he make to understand the message?
>> them that are weaned from the milk and drawn from the breasts?
>> for it is s-s, s-s,
>>> q-q, q-q,
>> a lad here (and) a lad there (28. 9–10).

The letters "s" and "q" occur together in this order in the Hebrew alphabet and the point of the taunt is that the prophet is like a teacher who thinks that it is his business to instruct grown-up men in their ABC.[1] It is safe to assume on this

[1] The usual translation, "precept upon precept; line upon line" is almost certainly wrong. The jingle must have sounded something like "saw lasaw, qaw, laqaw", as has been suggested by Professor G. R. Driver (to whom this paragraph is greatly indebted).

179

evidence that the Israelite teacher had his boys repeat in turn the letters of the alphabet, a suggestion which is confirmed by the word "alphabet" itself, which is associated with the Hebrew for groaning, moaning and muttering. It is not difficult to imagine the noisy sing-song of the scribe's class with its monotonous repetition of the same sounds.

Our ignorance of the average Israelite's educational attainment is equalled by our ignorance of that of more distinguished people, like prophets and kings. The book of Jeremiah, for example, makes it clear that the prophet dictated his teaching to his faithful secretary Baruch, but we have no means of knowing whether this was done as a simple convenience or an absolute necessity. The same is true of the other pre-exilic prophets. If, however, a man like Amos could not himself write, there must have been among his immediate disciples men who could, and who took the trouble to preserve his oracles as we now have them collected in a book.

Men who could not write, but who needed to transact official business, simply made their mark, just as "X his mark" passes for the signature of illiterate people today. The Israelites used for this purpose one of the letters of their alphabet which means a man's "mark" (see Job 31. 35) and which in ancient script looked very much like our "X". A far more common way of "signing" a document, however, was to seal it. Thus we read of Jeremiah's sealing a deed of purchase, when he bought some property in his native village (32. 10–14) and of Jezebel, who assumed her royal husband's authority and "wrote letters in Ahab's name, and sealed them with his seal" (I Kings 21. 8). The sealing of documents does not, of course, imply an inability to write (any more than it does today), but it is easy to see how much more important seals were in a society where writing was not a universal accomplishment. The essential point about a seal, then as now, is that it carries the authority of its owner and represents, so to speak, his legal "personality".

Hundreds of Palestinian seals and seal impressions from the period of the monarchy have been unearthed in recent excavations and they have provided a great deal of new information about many sides of everyday life. They have shed new light, for example, on the Israelite system of taxation (see pp. 167f.) and added to our knowledge (precious because it is so very small) of the work of Israelite artists (see pp. 207f.). The type of seal

180

86 A Cylinder-seal impression found at Uz, depicting the Mesopotamian idea of the creation of the world (*see p. 215*)

characteristic of this period was not the old cylinder type which was rolled on clay to make a "panel" impression (86, 114), but the flat signet, closely related to the Egyptian "scarab"—the seal shaped like the sacred beetle (*scarabaeus aegyptiorum*) of ancient Egypt. These scarab seals were generally made of semi-precious stones, with the engraving on the underside; sometimes, they were made into signet-rings (Genesis 41. 42).

Among the many finds, one of the most interesting is a seal impression discovered at Lachish in 1935. Its inscription reads: "Belonging to Gedaliah, the one who is over the house" and there is little doubt that it belonged to and was used by the Gedaliah who was made governor of Judah by the Babylonians after they had sacked Jerusalem in 586 B.C. Gedaliah was a member of a family of scribes who had distinguished themselves in the service of the State and here we find him sealing an official document. This near-approach to an Old Testament personality is rewarding enough, but the impression is valuable for yet another reason. On the back of the red clay, there is the clear imprint of the "weave" of the document to which it had been affixed. That document was clearly made of papyrus.

This evidence from Lachish, confirmed by a number of similar tell-tale imprints, enables us to say with confidence that papyrus was the common writing material in this period. None of it has survived the damp soil of Palestine (that is why we possess no ancient manuscripts of the Old Testament), but vast quantities have been preserved in the dry climate of Egypt, where it was used extensively for wrapping mummified bodies. It had been used as the scribe's "writing paper" in Egypt long before the Biblical period and was produced from the reed *cyperus papyrus*, which in ancient times grew in the region of the Nile. Palestinian papyrus may have been imported from Egypt, but as it now grows in northern Palestine, it is just possible that it was produced by the Israelites themselves.

Papyrus sheets for writing were made out of strips of the stem of the reed, first laid out in a row covering an area the size of the sheet required and then overlaid with cross strips. The two layers were then moistened, hammered out flat and dried in the sun. The off-white writing-surface (the upper one with the cross strips) was finally smoothed with some hard substance such as ivory or shell. Sometimes the papyrus was used in single sheets, measuring about 10×6 inches; sometimes the sheets were glued or sewn together to form a roll about thirty feet long. The two ends of the roll were sometimes attached to handles to make winding and unwinding easier; it must, nevertheless, have been extremely tedious when you wanted to look up a passage in a hurry. It was such a roll that Baruch made at Jeremiah's dictation and which was finally cut up and burnt in the king's brazier (Jeremiah 36). Books proper, that is to say, bound volumes with leaves, were not known until the Christian era and such libraries as the Israelites possessed (perhaps in scribal chambers in the Temple precincts) would consist of rolls, probably stored in wide-mouthed jars(68), like the recently-discovered Dead Sea documents.

Papyrus was the chief but not the only writing material. It is unlikely that clay tablets were used in this period, but animal skins were tanned for leather documents and wooden tablets were almost certainly used (Isaiah 8. 1; 30. 8). Above all, there is now abundant evidence to prove that bits of broken pottery (ordinary jugs and jars) were popular for short jottings, letters and business transactions. For example, over seventy such "ostraca" (that is, pieces of broken pottery used for writing) from eighth-century Samaria have been discovered. They deal with the supply of wine and oil and are almost certainly dockets recording the taxes in kind collected by the king (see pp. 166f.). They are written in ink in an easy flowing script and supply the earliest evidence we possess of the Hebrew dialect which was used in the Northern Kingdom. In other words, they give us a very good idea of what the book of the prophet Hosea must have looked like when it was first produced. Even more celebrated are the twenty-one letters which were discovered at Lachish in 1935 and 1938. Not all of them are legible, but those which can be read give a list of names and part of a correspondence between army officers in 589–8 B.C., when (in the words of the Old Testament) "the king of Babylon's army fought against Jerusalem, and against all the cities of Judah that were left, against Lachish and against Azekah" (Jeremiah 34. 7). The script of the ostraca is well executed and the style of the Hebrew prose may be compared to that which is found in the book of Jeremiah. The vividness with which these letters give us a glimpse of everyday life is increased by the fact that some of the pottery fragments can still be pieced together to make part of the wide-mouthed jar from which they originally came. Although we should find it extremely difficult to take notes on bits of broken crockery, it is not impossible that some of the sayings now preserved in the prophetic books were in the first place recorded by faithful disciples on such inconvenient writing material. Indeed, there is a tradition that Mohammed's followers copied their master's sayings on pieces of leather and bone and even on palm leaves. With our up-to-date typewriters, tape-recorders and printing presses, we tend not to marvel enough at the effort and ingenuity which were needed for preserving the spoken word and disseminating the written word in the ancient world.

It is possible to get a fair idea of the tools used by the Old Testament scribe from Egyptian sources. His pen was usually made of a reed with softened fibres at one end, so that it was more like a small paint brush than the hard-pointed pens we use, although it is clear that some writing-surfaces needed hard pens (see Jeremiah 17. 1). When papyrus or pottery was being used as the "paper", the letters were "painted" on to the writing-surface with deft strokes in black ink. We may well admire the quality of ink which has lasted nearly three thousand years. It seems to have been made of lamp-black and gum (occasionally with an iron compound added), and it was mixed as it was needed on a palette which the scribe carried about with him. His kit probably included a sponge for "rubbing out" mistakes and a knife for trimming the end of his pen (87).

183

87   An Israelite Scribe
and his kit

It is virtually certain that most of the writing in Old Testament times was the work of professional scribes and we should like to know much more about their organization. In ancient Egypt, scribes were systematically trained for their profession, and writing exercises of these students have been recovered. Some of them still show the teacher's marginal corrections and tell us enough to enable parts of the young scribes' syllabus to be reconstructed. It included a course in "commercial correspondence" and some of the pieces they were given to copy out were clearly intended to boost the scribal profession and to contrast it (not without black-coated snobbery) with the job of the manual worker (see Ecclesiasticus 38–9 for the Hebrew equivalent).   In the Old Testament, we hear most of the Hebrew scribes after the Exile, when they came to occupy a key position in the life of the people, as the students and teachers of religion. Even before the Exile, however, they rose to positions of prominence and became what we should call Secretaries of State (II Samuel 8. 17). They conducted the king's business, corresponded as Foreign Secretaries with their opposite numbers in other lands, and kept the national records—"the chronicles of the kings of Israel" and "the chronicles of the kings of Judah".   It would not be at all surprising if one day we discovered conclusive evidence to show that Jeremiah was not the only prophet to enjoy the services of a scribe, and that the literary achievement which the Old Testament represents owes, from the earliest times, more than the books themselves make plain to this educated and learned class of men.   As in the case of Gedaliah, the scribal profession ran in families (I Chronicles 2. 55) and it may even have had its own guild. Such a stable tradition would account for the remarkable fact that the script in which Hebrew was written remained virtually unchanged for nearly a thousand years.

Not all the scribes, however, were State officials and high-ranking civil servants. Some there must have been who were simply "writers"—clerks and secretaries, who (like modern shorthand-typists) took down dictation and wrote letters for their hard-earned living. These more humble scribes, like the letter-writers who can still be seen waiting to be hired in the streets of the East today, must have been the most familiar representatives of the profession to the ordinary Israelite as he went about his business.

EVERYDAY SCIENCE

Even when it is cautiously qualified, the term "science" is so blatantly wide of the mark in any account of Hebrew thought that it may be used without danger as a convenient way of grouping together a number of subjects which now properly fall into the scientific category. And not only now. Already in Old Testament times, the Babylonians were calculating the volume of pyramids, making astonishing strides in algebra, solving problems of surveying, compiling astronomical tables, listing and roughly classifying plants, animals, birds, fish and stones, and establishing formulae for metal alloys. Their capacity as observers merits the description of their achievement under such headings as mathematics, botany, zoology and mineralogy. Unless we count Solomon who (it is alleged) "spake of trees, from the cedar that is in Lebanon even unto the hyssop that springeth out of the wall . . . also of beasts, and of fowl, and of creeping things, and of fishes" (I Kings 4. 33), the Israelites have nothing to offer which is even vaguely comparable. As the great Oriental scholar, William Robertson Smith, observed a long time ago, the Hebrew "values nature only in so far as it moves and affects him, or is capable of being moved and affected by him . . . to him nature is what he feels as he beholds it". Such imperious subjectivity is not the foundation on which the natural sciences are built.

(i) *The Universe*

Although the Hebrews' main interest in the universe was characteristically a belief about it—the belief that it had been made by a good God and belonged to him (which is the point of the unscientific parables of Creation at the beginning of Genesis), all the Old Testament writers take for granted the rough cosmology which is sketched in the diagram (88). It is very much like other Mesopotamian conceptions of the universe and very different from our own (if, indeed, most of us can be

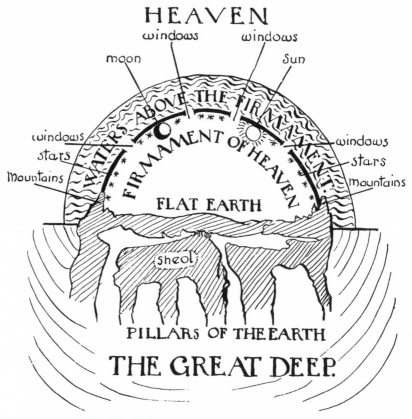

HEAVEN

88 The Hebrew conception of the Universe

said to have one at all). The three stories into which it is divided are clearly stated in the familiar words of the Second Commandment: "Thou shalt not make unto thee a graven image, nor the likeness of any form that is in *heaven above*, or that is in the *earth beneath*, or that is in *the water under the earth*" (Exodus 20. 4). The earth, which is round and flat, occupies the centre of the world. Over it, is stretched a solid dome, the firmament of heaven, firmly resting on the mountain-pillars round the edge of the earth. On the inner side of this dome, the sun, the moon and the stars move in their proper courses. On the other side of the dome (that is, in the area which was thought of as Heaven) are the "waters above the firmament", originally part of the ocean of primeval Chaos,

186

before it was divided into two at the creation of the world. Instead of flooding the earth, these upper waters now supply rain, snow and hail through the "windows of heaven". Beneath the earth also, there is a mighty ocean—the Great Deep, which the Hebrew imagination conceived of as being permitted at times to resume its former supremacy and reduce the world to Chaos. The story of the Flood is introduced with the words: "on the same day were all the fountains of the great deep broken up, and the windows of heaven were opened" (Genesis 7. 11). Normally, however, the Great Deep was confined to its ordained bounds beneath the earth. The earth itself rests firmly on pillars formed of mountains sunk in the subterranean waters and only in exceptional circumstances are these foundations shaken. Also in this lower region, there is *Sheol* (less localized than the diagram suggests), the gloomy abode of the dead.

This simple model of the universe displays no scientific curiosity, but it does demonstrate that principle of God-maintained order in the world, which underlies the whole of Old Testament thought and is so magnificently affirmed in Psalm 104. This conception of order sprang from the Hebrews' religious awareness and, despite the unscientific way in which it is expounded, the scientist of the twentieth century might profitably meditate on its far-reaching implications.

(ii) *The Calendar*

The Israelites' notion of time and its division into years, months and weeks also show how little they were concerned with abstract speculation. The "clock-time" to which we are all enslaved, with its remorselessly fixed units of hours and minutes, was in no way envisaged by them. Even the suggestion, based on the text of II Kings 20. 9–11, that the king of Judah kept his eye on a sundial akin to the ancient Egyptian shadow-clocks, rests on flimsy evidence; the Hebrew means no more than the shadow made by the sun on "steps"—perhaps those of the royal palace. The Israelites thought of time in terms of its *content* rather than of its length. Thus, when they spoke of harvest-time, it was of the harvest itself that they were thinking and not of a bit of the calendar about September and October. When we speak of time vaguely, and ask somebody to come and see us "before lunch" or "after the holidays", we most nearly approach the more leisurely outlook of the Old Testament world, when it didn't matter if dinner *was* kept waiting and when the arrival of a guest was likely to be long remembered as a red-letter day. Time was thus arranged round significant happenings; the Israelites were entirely free from the joint tyranny of punctuality and engagement books.

Even the Israelites, however, were regulated by the rhythm of the seasons. Only four of the ancient names for the months of the year have survived and, as we should expect, they refer to what was then happening in the world of Nature. Thus, *Abib*, the first month of spring, corresponding to our March–April, means "month of the ears" and *Ziw*, the following month, means the "month of bright flowers". The month itself was determined, not by any mathematical division of the year into units, but by observation of the moon. When the new moon was seen (and it must have been easy to miss it in cloudy weather), a new month began. Unfortunately, the natural year does not divide neatly into an exact number of lunar months, being about eleven days longer than twelve of them. As the months were associated with particular seasons, it must have been necessary every two or three years to add an extra (thirteenth) month. Otherwise, the "month of bright flowers" would have slipped back into winter and then into summer until, after about thirty-three years, it regained its proper position in spring. After the Exile, when an attempt was made to regularize the calendar, the old names of the months were abandoned and, instead, they were numbered from 1 to 12, beginning with the new moon of spring. In this period, however, the new year was generally considered to begin at the autumn equinox, which was referred to as "the going out" and "the return" of the year (Exodus 23. 16; 34. 22).

89 An ivory Tablet, used, perhaps, as a monthly Calendar

Just as the month in Old Testament times was determined independently of the year, so the week bore no simple relationship to the month. The seven-day week may originally have been suggested by the four phases of the moon, but as a lunar month consists of about $29\frac{1}{2}$ days, weeks and months could never be in step. The Israelites, who came to attach great

188

importance to the seventh day of the week—the sabbath (the only day, incidentally, which had a name)—never tried to regulate the relationship between the two. As in our own calendar, the first day of the month could fall on any day of the week. It is possible that at one time the month was split up into three "decades" of days and that the bone and ivory tablets punctured with thirty holes arranged in three columns of ten, which have been found in the excavations, were calendars (89). This method of dividing the month, deriving from Egypt, cannot have been either widespread or long-lived. It is, indeed, possible that the thirty-day "calendars" were markers for some totally different purpose.

The Israelites' lack of precision in reckoning time seems to have extended even to the definition of a day. The common one was certainly the working day from dawn to sunset, but perhaps, even before the Exile, a day was thought of as extending from sunset to sunset, as it was in New Testament times. This rather curious notion may be accounted for by the fact that the Hebrew month began with the observation of the new moon in the evening and not unnaturally a new month was held to begin with a new day. The Israelites' day was not portioned out in hours and minutes (for which Hebrew has no words), but practical considerations led them to divide the night into three watches.

(iii) *Weights and Measures*

Considering their lack of interest in mathematics and precise reckoning, we are not surprised to learn that the science of metrology was singularly undeveloped among the Israelites. Their weights and measures varied from city to city and it is impossible to reduce our fragmentary evidence into anything approaching a reliable and coherent system. The Chronicler, it is true, credits the Levites with official responsibility for "all manner of measure and size" (I Chronicles 23. 29), and the collection of taxes under the monarchy seems to have stimulated some degree of standardization, but the picture still remains one of great variety.

The basic unit of weight was the *shekel*, a term which derives from the verb meaning "to weigh" in all Semitic languages. When the prophet asked who had "weighed the mountains in scales, and the hills in a balance?" (Isaiah 40. 12), he was

189

90, 91 Inscribed stone Weights

drawing his metaphor from one of the most common sights of the market-place. The balances used for weighing precious metals were not very different in design from the type still used(20). As may be seen from the Egyptian illustration, weights were often made in the shape of animals, but the Israelite specimens were simpler and cruder. Most of them were balls of limestone and some of the excavated examples bear rough inscriptions or markings to indicate their value.

On the two examples in the illustration (90, 91), the mark which resembles a figure 8 with the top cut off is generally thought to represent the standard shekel and the other sign the numeral 8. It is difficult to co-ordinate such evidence with the Biblical data, but the following table will serve as a rough guide:

> 1 shekel = 2/5 ounce (approx. 11·4 grammes)
> 50 shekels = 1 mina = 20 ounces (571 grammes)
> 60 minas = 1 talent = 75 pounds (34,000 grammes)

In this period, coined money had not been invented and all business transactions were done either by barter (so many sheep in exchange for so much grain, etc.), or by the payment of a given weight of silver or gold. Thus, Abraham, in buying the cave of Machpelah, is said to have "weighed to Ephron . . . four hundred shekels of silver, *current with the merchant*" (Genesis 23. 16). Payment in metal was obviously less clumsy than payment in kind, but (as the last words of the quotation indicate) it was necessary to make sure of its quality. When coinage proper was introduced at a later period, its stamp guaranteed both the quality and the quantity of the metal.

The measurement of capacity likewise remains obscure, although in a country of which the chief products (corn, oil and wine) were sold and taken as taxes by volume, there must have been some degree of standardization, if only on a regional basis. In this sphere, the most interesting contribution from archaeology is the top of a storage jar from eighth-century Lachish, on which there had been incised before firing the

92 The top of a Storage Jar, with the inscription "royal bath"

190

inscription "bath la-melekh", meaning "royal bath"(92). The *bath* (pronounced with a short "a") was a liquid measure and it has been calculated that this particular jar held about twenty-two litres. Other jars bearing a more elaborate royal stamp and probably used for the king's taxes were almost certainly twice the size (see p. 167). Different but related measures were used for liquids and dry-stuffs, the principal ones being as follows:

Dry			*Liquid*		
1 omer	$=\frac{1}{2}$ gallon (2·3 litres)		1 hin	$=5/6$ gallon (3·8 litres)	
10 omers	$=1$ ephah $=5$ gallons		6 hins	$=1$ bath $=5$ gallons	
10 ephahs	$=1$ homer $=50$ gallons		10 baths	$=1$ kor $=50$ gallons	

When Amos found the wheat merchants "making the ephah small, and the shekel great, and dealing falsely with balances of deceit" (8. 5), he castigated them for giving small measure and weighing for themselves too much silver in payment. Israelite linear measurement was even more obviously un-theoretical. Its four units were based on a man's arms and hands:

$$1 \text{ finger} = \tfrac{3}{4} \text{ inch}$$
$$4 \text{ fingers} = 1 \text{ palm} = 3 \text{ inches}$$
$$3 \text{ palms} = 1 \text{ span} = 9 \text{ inches}$$
$$2 \text{ spans} = 1 \text{ cubit} = 18 \text{ inches}$$

The span was measured from the tip of the thumb to the tip of the little finger when the hand was spread out and the cubit from the elbow to the tip of the second finger. The Siloam tunnel has a famous inscription (given on p. 137) stating that its length was 1200 cubits. Its measurement after excavation has established the value of the cubit there used as roughly equivalent to $17\frac{1}{2}$ inches.

Greater lengths and areas were indicated in the most practical way possible. Laban, for example, "set three days' journey betwixt himself and Jacob" (Genesis 30. 36). Again, in Isaiah 5. 10 ("ten acres of vineyard shall yield one bath"), the word translated "acre" means properly a yoke of two oxen, and, by extension, the amount of land they can plough in a day. The prophet is describing a crop failure and using the language of the working farmer. It is still dimly echoed when a gardener today speaks not of so many square yards, but of a "day's digging".

MEDICINE

Medicine in the ancient Near East was a curious combination of genuine acuteness in observing curative methods which actually worked, and rank superstition. Both elements are to be found in Hebrew medical practice, but the Israelites' dominating belief in a single all-governing God had a profound influence in reducing the magical element. However, in so far as it meant that every condition of man, whether in sickness or in health, was directly ascribed to the action of God, this belief also tended to hold up the development of professional medicine on a rational and scientific basis. When a Hebrew writer could say in God's name, "I kill, and I make alive; I have wounded, and I heal" (Deuteronomy 32. 39), little scope appeared to be left for the skill of the doctor.

The prevailing idea of sickness in the Old Testament was that God sent it as a punishment for sin, although from time to time there arose men (like the author of the book of Job), who courageously challenged this terrible notion, and insisted that some sufferers were undoubtedly innocent. When physical and mental afflictions were not ascribed to God directly, they were attributed to the diabolic work of demons and evil spirits. For the ordinary Hebrew, the air was thick with these hostile supernatural agents and they could only be met on their own level by rituals, charms and incantations, which survived in popular religion, despite the explicit disapproval of Israel's spiritual leaders. The Brazen Serpent of Numbers 21. 8f. was thought to have magical properties and many of the clay plaques and figurines which archaeologists have unearthed were clearly intended for the sick-room(59, 117). It is also highly probable that some of the "curses", which are so disturbing a feature of many of the Psalms, were hurled not against human enemies but against the demons of disease. They represent, that is to say, primitive medicine rather than primitive religion. When today we speak of a person's having a "stroke", we still echo the ancient notion of supernatural affliction. It is really not surprising that in a pre-scientific era people suffering from mental disorders and delirious fevers, who were obviously "beside themselves", should have been thought to be victims of demon possession. Inevitably, the Israelites regarded lunatics with a mixture of pity and fear—an attitude which

David once exploited, when he pretended to be mad before the king of Gath (I Samuel 21. 12–15). Nor is it surprising that the rapid and devastating spread of epidemics before anything like inoculations or disinfectants had been invented should have helped to confirm the ancient belief in collective punishment.

When a man fell ill in Old Testament times, he went either to the local sanctuary (as he would have done in Egypt or in Babylon, where medical practice was in the hands of the priest-hood), or, if he were lucky enough to be in touch with a "holy man" (rather misleadingly called a "prophet" in the Old Testament), appeal would be made to him. The strange figure of Elisha is the nearest approximation to a family doctor provided by the Old Testament books. The circles from which we have received our information about him certainly thought that he was capable of transferring leprosy from one person to another (II Kings 5. 27), of disinfecting the local water supply (2. 20ff.) and of ridding food of poison (4. 41). He was the obvious person to be consulted by a foreign king when he fell sick (8. 7ff.) and it is recorded that he brought a dead boy back to life (4. 22–37). This last incident, in which Elisha performed various acts of sympathetic magic (not artificial respiration!), very strongly resembles common ritual practices in neighbouring countries of the Near East. Many other illustrations of the power of the "prophet" over life and death may be found in the Old Testament, but in the circle of the great prophets (like Amos, Isaiah and Jeremiah), such powers were definitely depreciated and all the emphasis is placed on their proper work of being God's spokesmen to the people.

Nevertheless, it is from Isaiah that we get one of the clearest examples of a Hebrew medical prescription. When king Hezekiah was suffering from a boil, the prophet prescribed a poultice of figs, as a result of which the patient recovered (II Kings 20. 7). Evidently, the fig was a popular remedy, if we may judge by a veterinary prescription from Ras Shamra. It advocated that figs should be given (through the nose!) to ailing horses, which was, apparently, common practice in North Syria 800 years before Hezekiah got his boil.

The case of another royal patient suggests that eventually some medical men were able to establish themselves and win their independence of the religious authorities. The Chronicler records that "in the thirty and ninth year of his reign Asa was diseased in his feet; his disease was exceeding great: yet in his disease he sought not to the Lord, but to the physicians" (II Chronicles 16. 12). We should like to know not only what the physicians did for the king's gout, but also what their status was in society. The Code of Hammurabi (about 1700 B.C.; see p. 30) makes it plain that many centuries earlier in Babylon, the medical profession was highly organized and governed not only by a strict code of professional etiquette, but also by a standard scale of fees. There is nothing to correspond to this in the Hebrew codes of law, although the provision of Exodus 21. 19 may well mean that after a brawl between two men, the victim who was awarded "costs" could make his assailant pay the surgeon's bill. This, however, is only a scrap of evidence and we must conclude that medical services in Israel were at best scanty.

The Israelites were certainly ignorant of any scientific medicine, and such knowledge as they possessed was of the practical kind which is learnt by trial and error. For example, the firm belief that a dead body must on no account be tampered with absolutely excluded the possibility of dissection and, therefore, any advance in the knowledge of anatomy. The Egyptians were not so restricted and in consequence their knowledge was much more scientific.

Despite such drawbacks, practical experience supplied the Israelites with some genuine, if unsystematic, information. The religious legislation about leprosy (if, indeed, that is the proper identification of the disease) in Leviticus 13 obviously assumes that the priests had more than a little ability in diagnosis. And the story of the Philistines, who sacrificed five golden mice to stay the bubonic plague (I Samuel 6), not only reflects primitive magical notions, but also an awareness that the contagion is carried by flea-infested rodents. The same curious mixture of magic and empirical knowledge is confirmed by the remedies which were kept in the Israelites' medicine-chest. The resinous gum from Gilead ("the balm of Gilead"), wormwood, gall-water (presumably a concoction of bitter herbs), and various oils had clearly proved their value in actual experience, but the mandrake was popular more for its supposed magical qualities than for its medicinal value. There is a similar ambiguity about the use of the liver of animals and fish.

No matter for what mysterious reasons this particular medicine commended itself to the ancient world, a population reared on codliver oil is in no position to be contemptuous of its use. We do not know whether the invalid diet of little cakes mentioned in II Samuel 13. 6–8 had any nutritive or curative properties, but as their Hebrew name discloses the fact that they were heart-shaped, we may at least conclude that they were strongly suggestive.

Internal disorders and infections are obviously more easily exploited by magic-mongers than cuts and wounds and so it is not surprising that (according to our evidence) the Israelites achieved more in the latter sphere of medicine than in any other. When God is referred to as a "healer" (as in Job 5. 18 and Psalm 103. 3), it is the surgeon who is most often in the writer's mind. The historian records in a matter-of-fact way that "king Joram returned to be healed in Jezreel of the wounds which the Syrians had given him at Ramah" (II Kings 8. 29) and Isaiah draws on the familiar language of surgery to describe the plight of his people: "From the sole of the foot even unto the head there is no soundness in it; but wounds, and bruises, and fresh stripes: they have not been squeezed, neither bound up, neither mollified with oil" (1. 6). Elijah sheds a stray beam of light on the provisions made for the lame. His familiar challenge—"How long halt ye between two opinions?" may be translated literally, "How long do you hobble between two crutches?" and so evidently battle-scarred warriors and old men on wooden crutches were a feature of the everyday scene.

We know for certain that Hebrew surgeons went beyond simply patching up the maimed and conducted full-scale operations. Excavations at Lachish have disclosed a great number of human skulls, among which were three cases of "trepanning", the operation which involves either boring through the skull bone or sawing away a part of it to relieve pressure on the brain. One skull, belonging to the eighth century B.C., shows evidence that the patient survived the operation long enough for new bone to grow and almost obliterate the marks of the surgeon's saw. When we consider the crudeness of the surgeon's instruments and the lack of all antiseptics and anaesthetics, the terror of undergoing an operation in Old Testament times hardly bears thinking about. We know nothing, incidentally, of Israelite dentists. As early as the fifth century B.C., the Phoenicians were making false teeth, but it is unlikely that even the kings of Israel enjoyed such refinements.

If we read some of the pitiful psalms which describe bodily sickness (for example, Psalms 6, 22, 88, 102), we shall receive a vivid impression of the horrors of ill-health in a country which inevitably exposed its inhabitants to physical hardship, and in which suffering was regarded as a disgrace. Apart from the bubonic plague, which was the scourge of the Near East, the most common afflictions must have been skin diseases and eye troubles caused by dust, flies and the merciless glare of the sun. Sunstroke was probably responsible for the death of the boy who went out with his father to reap in the fields and suddenly cried out, "My head, my head" (II Kings 4. 18f.). Droughts brought famine in their train, and malnutrition and sheer starvation must have taken a heavy toll of life among the peasants. Inadequate and foul water-supplies were the breeding-ground of fevers, and are probably to be held responsible for the various digestive disorders which are alluded to more than once in the books of the Old Testament. For obvious reasons, the specific diseases of ancient Israel are difficult and often impossible to identify. Our information about the conditions of health in Egypt, for example, is much more complete, not only because various important medical papyri have survived, but for the remarkable reason that it is still possible to conduct post-mortem examinations on Egyptian mummies. As a result of these grim investigations, it is disconcerting to discover that the Egyptians were familiar with poliomyelitis and tuberculosis. It may safely be assumed that the Israelites were in the same position.

It is pleasing to be able to conclude this sketch of suffering by recalling a nice touch of ordinary humanity. When Hezekiah had recovered from his boil (thanks to Isaiah and his fig poultice), he received a deputation sent from the court of Babylon to congratulate him on his return to health. Now the king was up and about again, he took great pleasure in showing his well-wishers round his palace: "At that time Merodach-baladan the son of Baladan, king of Babylon, sent letters and a present to Hezekiah: for he heard that he had been sick, and was recovered. And Hezekiah was glad of them, and shewed them the house of his spicery, the silver, and the gold, and the spices, and the precious oil, and all the house of his jewels, and

all that was found in his treasures" (Isaiah 39.1f.). So exhaustive
a conducted tour provides ample evidence that the patient had
fully recovered his strength.

MUSIC

The popularity and importance of music-making in ancient
Israel and the esteem in which music-makers were held are
disclosed by the fact that musicians come second in the three
classes into which the tradition of Genesis divides mankind—
owners of flocks and herds, musicians and metal workers
(Genesis 4. 20ff.). And all the books of the Old Testament tell
the same story. They are full of references to singing, dancing
and music. Every special occasion had its proper musical
accompaniment, from the gay to the grave—feasts, weddings
and funerals. Victorious warriors returning from the battlefield
were welcomed home by excited processions of singers, and
music was an essential ingredient of the parties held to give
friends and relations a good send-off.

There is no doubt that the Israelites, like other ancient
peoples, thought of music as possessing a mysterious quality
capable of making a difference in the supernatural world; it
drove away evil spirits and attracted the spirit of prophecy.
It could be either soothing or invigorating. David played to
Saul to quieten him in a mood of agitation and black despair;
while, on the other hand, bands of "prophets" worked themselves up into a frenzy with "a psaltery, and a timbrel, and a
pipe, and a harp" (I Samuel 10. 5).

Music, however, was not simply a matter of psychotherapy
or prophetic ecstasy. David's skill as a musician earned him
the reputation of being the author of the Psalms, and the
organizer of an elaborate Temple choir. Although we cannot
accept this enthusiastic legend simply as it stands, it is more than
likely that the famous tradition of Hebrew liturgical music was
established under the patronage of David and Solomon. There
is clear evidence to show that the Jews were renowned far and
wide for their musical ability. After the fall of Jerusalem, for
example, the Israelite exiles in Babylon were asked by their
captors to sing one of the "songs of Zion" (Psalm 137); and
earlier, when the Assyrian king Sennacherib was able to exact
tribute from Hezekiah, he was enlightened enough to demand
"his male and female musicians" and to boast of the acquisition

in his annals. Evidently, professional musicians were kept at the court in Jerusalem in 700 B.C.

We should, of course, like to know what ancient Hebrew music sounded like, but historical sources, however faithful they may be, are silent witnesses. The Israelites had no musical notation and so the best way of trying to get some kind of sound-picture is to discover as exactly as possible what instruments they normally used and what is the music of the most isolated Jewish communities and of other Semitic peoples at the present day. Even the identification of their instruments is precarious, for the wood, leather and gut of which they were made have all long since perished (93–102).

A start may be made with two of the Old Testament passages which give a list of instruments. In II Samuel 6. 5, which describes how David brought the Ark of God to Jerusalem, we are told that it was greeted with "harps, and with psalteries, and with timbrels, and with castanets, and with cymbals". And in Psalm 150, it is implied that the Temple music was supplied by the trumpet, the psaltery, the harp, the timbrel, the pipe, the "loud cymbals" and the "high-sounding cymbals".

What strikes us immediately in these two lists is the abundance of percussion instruments. The modern jazz enthusiast would have appreciated the accent on rhythm, and would (quite rightly) have come to the conclusion that a great deal of Hebrew music, both religious and popular, was *dance* music. The instrument called (in the Revised Version) the "timbrel" (or "tabret") was a *hand drum*. It was normally played by the womenfolk and consisted of two skins stretched over a wooden hoop frame. Probably it lacked the jingling metal pieces of the tambourine, and its sound must have been rather similar to that of a tom-tom. The *cymbals* almost explain themselves. They were made of metal and (as their Hebrew name suggests) gave out a clashing or a jingling sound. Apparently, there were two distinct kinds. The "loud cymbals" were struck together vertically and made a harsh crashing noise, which could hardly be called a musical sound at all, while the "high-sounding cymbals" were struck horizontally (like hand-clapping) and gave a clear ringing note. The other percussion instrument used by David's procession was what the Revised Version calls "castanets", or, in the marginal reading, "sistra". The Hebrew name suggests shaking or rattling and there is little doubt that

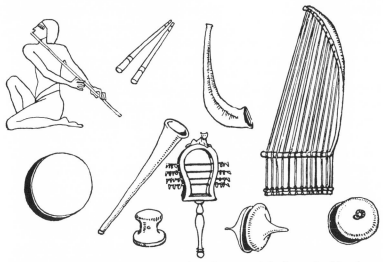

93–102 Musical Instruments: *reading from top left*, flute, double oboe, ram's horn trumpet, harp (Assyrian); *reading from bottom left*, hand drum, metal trumpet, rattle, sistrum, loud cymbals, high-sounding cymbals

the *sistrum* of Egyptian origin is meant. The sistrum looks rather like the oval frame of a hand-mirror. Thick wires were threaded across the frame through holes on each side of it; they were left loose in the holes, so that when the instrument was shaken, it made a metallic rattle. It is possible that the same Hebrew word was used for many different kinds of *rattle*; some have recently been excavated at Debir. These specimens are made of clay and look rather like stubby hour-glasses. They are hollow and contain a pebble. Anybody who has heard Latin-American music (and who in these days has not?) will know how rattles are used and what kind of din they make.

After the percussion instruments, the string section must be reviewed. Scholars tell us firmly that we must give up the traditional idea that David played a harp; his instrument was the *lyre*. The Hebrew name (*kinnor*) was what the Greeks and Romans called "cithara" and its identification is almost certain. It is even possible that we have a picture of ancient Hebrews using this particular instrument. The Asiatic lyre-player entering Egypt, who is depicted on the Beni-Hasan tomb painting(11), gives us a very good idea of what a nomadic Israelite lyre-player looked like, and we also possess a relief from Assyria, which

199

shows a number of lyre-players who, in all probability, were Israelite captives. The strings of the lyre were stretched across the sounding-board and the space between the two "arms" of the instrument and were then attached to a sort of cross-bar at the top. The frame was made of wood (usually cypress) and the strings of thin sheep gut, known as "chitterlings". The player either struck all the strings with a plectrum and prevented some of them from sounding by touching them as he struck with the finger-tips of the left hand, or else, when playing a solo, plucked the strings with his right hand.

Although David's *kinnor*, usually translated harp, was really a lyre, the "psaltery" mentioned in both lists of instruments was probably a *harp* of some kind. The Hebrew name for this harp—*nebel*—is the ordinary word for a skin bottle, and this gives a clue about its appearance. We must put out of our minds the large stately harps we now see on concert platforms (which always look exceedingly heavy and rest on the ground), and think instead of a small instrument which would be played as it was carried about. According to our modern notions, it was held upside down, that is, with its sound-box on top. Closely associated with the harp is the Hebrew word *asor*, which means "ten". It may simply describe the harp as "an instrument of ten strings", or (as some think) another instrument altogether. One of the foremost authorities on Hebrew music is of the opinion that it refers to the *zither* of Phoenician origin, an instrument which looks very much like an empty picture frame, with ten strings stretched across it.

Now the wind instruments. Of these, the most important was the *trumpet*. Again, there were two kinds: the trumpet made out of a straightened ram's horn and the trumpet made of metal. The ram's horn trumpet is the only ancient musical instrument still used by the Jews today. It is sounded, for example, at the end of the New Year festival and on the Day of Atonement. In some ways, it has little claim to be regarded as a musical instrument. It was used rather as we fire guns or ring church bells—not to play tunes but to give signals (like a hunting horn), and to announce national events, such as the outbreak of war, the coronation of a king, and the greater religious festivals. What it lacked in tone, it made up in volume. Little wonder that popular tradition had it that the walls of Jericho were shattered by its blasts (Joshua 6). The metal trumpets

200

are almost always mentioned in the plural (like the two silver trumpets ascribed to Moses in Numbers 10) and this suggests that they were probably played together, perhaps in fanfares. There remains to be mentioned the "pipe". The Hebrew word usually translated "pipe" literally means "pierced". It may refer to any kind of wood-wind instrument, but the likelihood is that it means the *double oboe*, which was common in the ancient Near East. Shepherds must have played *flutes* in ancient Israel as they do today, but, oddly enough, there is no certain reference to them in the Old Testament. Possibly, the pipe mentioned in Genesis 4. 21 is the flute; at least, the Hebrew word here is connected with the idea of being in love, and the hollow OO-sound made in pronouncing it may give us an idea of the note of the instrument.[1]

Hand drum, cymbals, sistrum, rattles, lyre, harp, zither, trumpet, double oboe and (probably) flute: such were the instruments in the Hebrew orchestra (93–102). But "orchestra" is rather misleading, for it is unlikely that all these instruments were ever formed into a single unit for concert playing; the trumpets, for example, were probably never used in this way. The other instruments could be, but were not necessarily all employed simultaneously; and unlike instruments in the orchestra we know, the wind instruments and the string instruments probably all played essentially the same tune, so that there was no harmony such as we are accustomed to in orchestral playing. Instruments were primarily used singly or in small ensembles for the accompaniment of singing (they were significantly called "tools of singing") and it is improbable that there was much either unaccompanied singing or music without words.

A great deal of the Israelites' singing, like that of many primitive peoples today, was antiphonal, that is, it was divided between two groups of voices, or a solo-voice and a group of voices, who "answered" each other alternately. The structure of the Psalms obviously invites this kind of singing, since each verse divides in the middle and a parallel statement is made in the second half. For example, in Psalm 8. 4:

> What is man, that thou art mindful of him?
> And the son of man, that thou visitest him?

[1] See *The Biblical Archaeologist*, September 1941, for a valuable article by O. R. Sellers, to which this section owes much.

We associate antiphonal singing with religious services; but a few of our folksongs are antiphonal (like "Green grow the rushes-o!") and the Israelites adopted it spontaneously on every kind of occasion. For example, we read in I Samuel 18. 6f. that "when David returned from the slaughter of the Philistines ... the women came out of all the cities of Israel, singing and dancing, to meet king Saul, with timbrels, with joy, and with instruments of music. And the women *sang one to another* in their play, and said,

> Saul hath slain his thousands,
> And David his ten thousands".

The nature of their singing as antiphonal is made quite plain here by the Revised Version's alternative reading of *answered one another* for "sang one to another".

Both singers and instrumentalists inherited traditional tunes on which they freely improvised variations. We know from the headings of the psalms that there were some good old favourites. Such mysterious words in these headings as "For the Chief Musician; set to Shushan Eduth" (Psalm 60), "For the Chief Musician; set to Jonath elem rehokim" (Psalm 56), and "For the Chief Musician; set to Aijeleth hash-Shahar" (Psalm 22) refer to the names of well-known tunes. Thus Psalm 60 is to be sung to the tune called "The lily of testimony"; Psalm 56 to "The silent dove of them that are afar off"; and Psalm 22 to "The hind of the morning". Originally, these were the titles of songs which established themselves in popular favour and of which the tunes were borrowed for use with different words— even the words of psalms. We can find much the same sort of thing in our own hymn books, where certain hymns are put down to such tunes as "Duke Street" ("Fight the good fight") or "Cwm Rhondda" ("Guide me, O thou great Redeemer").

The tunes in Old Testament times were almost certainly built up from a small number of stock musical phrases, as the musical reader may judge by the example shown on the opposite page(103). This music is used in the Yemenite community, which is one of a few small groups of Jewish people who have been isolated for centuries, and who may well have kept up the old tunes unchanged since the time of Jeremiah.

103   A traditional Jewish Tune

Anybody who has ever heard plainsong will have some idea of the sound of ancient Hebrew chanting. We can get some idea of what the Hebrew "orchestra" sounded like by listening to Arabic music on one or other of the Middle Eastern radio programmes.

Although we have to recreate and imagine as best we can the music of Hebrew songs, we are still able to read their words. That magnificent collection we know as the Psalter, of course, springs to mind immediately, but it is clear that other song-books existed. We hear, for example, of *The Book of Jashar* (or, the Upright) in II Samuel 1. 18 and of *The Book of the Wars of the Lord* in Numbers 21. 14. It would be inaccurate to say that the latter book (now lost to us) was non-religious, because nearly every bit of everyday life in Old Testament times was related, however indirectly, to religious beliefs and practices. But, at least, we may say that the war pieces it contained were sung outside religious services. Of the Israelites' war songs, we possess the splendid victory hymns of Deborah (Judges 5) and Miriam (Exodus 15. 20f.) and another fragment may be found in Joshua 10. 12f. No funeral service in this period was complete without mourning songs, which were usually sung by professionals. They can be sampled at their very best in David's lament on the death of Saul and Jonathan ("The Song of the Bow") in the first chapter of II Samuel. Again, weddings called for singing and in Psalm 45, for example, we possess an anthem composed for a royal marriage.

But not all (or even most) Hebrew songs were set pieces of outstanding literary merit. Above all, men sang at their work. The Old Testament contains many echoes of rhythmic pieces which were sung as the grapes were trampled in the wine-press. "Music While You Work" to speed up production was not entirely an invention of the BBC in the twentieth century! And then, we have a pleasant little snatch of a song sung by a grape-gatherer at work in the vineyard:

Catch for us the foxes,
The tiny, little foxes;
For they ruin all our vineyards,
When our vineyards are in bloom

(Song of Songs 2. 15).

To judge by the reference in Isaiah 21. 11f., the night-watchman was also in the habit of singing to keep himself cheerful as he went on his rounds in the city. To give the other side of the picture, there is a song reflected in Nehemiah 4. 10, which is not so much a song of men at work, as a vocal complaint of workers on strike!

Drinking-songs were as popular among the Israelites as they were supposed to be among continental university students in the good old romantic days of the last century. "Let us eat and drink, for tomorrow we shall die", which is the characteristic theme of them all, is to be found in so many words in Isaiah 22. 13. No doubt hearty choruses of this kind helped revellers to turn night into day at many a wild party, when the harvest was being gathered, or the sheep had been sheared. Then, of course, many popular "numbers" must have added to the general hilarity and we can guess that these (no less than their twentieth-century counterparts) rang the changes on the Hebrew equivalents of such words as "love" and "dove" and "dear" and "near". The best Old Testament love songs come from the period after the Exile (for example, Song of Songs, 1. 9–17; 2. 8–14), but there is every reason for supposing that the younger generation had amused themselves with similar ditties for centuries. At least, the prophet Ezekiel bitterly reflected that people took about as much notice of what he had to say as they did of the singers of love ballads; he might just as well have been "one that hath a pleasant voice, and can play well on an instrument" (Ezekiel 33. 32). That is the nearest approach we can make to the Israelite "vocalist".

ART

One of the biggest handicaps in grasping imaginatively what everyday life was like in Old Testament times is that the Israelites have left us no pictorial records. There is nothing to compare, for example, with the mural reliefs from Assyria or the Egyptian tomb paintings. Art, in the narrow sense of painting and sculpture, was not one of their achievements.

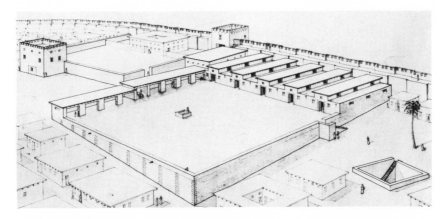

104 A reconstruction of some of Solomon's stables at Megiddo (*see pp. 66f.*)

105   The excavated remains of Solomon's stables at Megiddo, with their
stone tie-posts and mangers

MEGIDDO

106   A large official building with a watch-tower built by Solomon at Megiddo

The fact that kings and nobles went to the trouble of importing foreign craftsmen to build and decorate their houses shows, however, that the Israelites as a people cannot be said to have been insensitive to artistic considerations, and suggests that it was poverty more than anything else which held up the development of a native art.

Another reason may be found in the Second Commandment: "Thou shalt not make unto thee a graven image, nor the likeness of any form that is in heaven above, or that is in the earth beneath, or that is in the water under the earth: thou shalt not bow down thyself unto them, nor serve them." It is not easy to determine the exact scope of this injunction. Taken literally, the first part of it would appear to prohibit pictorial representation of any visible object whatsoever—a very sweeping law indeed. It is probable, however, that this first part should be interpreted in the light of the final statement and that the intention was to forbid any pictorial representation made *in order that it should be worshipped.* At a later period, the commandment was interpreted as prohibiting the representation of any *living creature*, but as saying nothing about (and, therefore, allowing) the representation of natural objects like flowers and trees. Whatever the exact interpretation of the commandment in Old Testament times, there is little doubt that it acted as a damper on the development of all forms of art. It did not, of course, influence those who cared little for the tradition of Moses, and of such renegades, archaeologists have proved that there was a considerable number. But the hundreds of clay figurines which have been unearthed in Palestine have no claim to be ranked as works of art. They are mass-produced objects and, for the most part, as crude artistically as the superstitions they were made to serve(59, 117). The noblest and highest religion of Israel was of the kind which expressed itself in moral fervour and courageous faith rather than in artistic creation.

The Israelites, nevertheless, did reveal artistic skill and appreciation in two subsidiary art forms—gem-cutting and interior decorating. As recent excavations have cast light on both, they are worth brief consideration. Of the two, gem-cutting is nearer everyday life, because it was practised mainly in the making of the personal seals with which all official business was transacted. Most of them were made of semi-precious stones (like agate) and many of them included in their design, not only

107 The Seal of Shema, officer of Jeroboam II

personal names in the old Hebrew script, but finely-cut figures of recognizable animals or mythical beings like sphinxes. Of the first category, two particularly good examples have been discovered. The earlier one was found at Megiddo and its inscription, "Belonging to Shema, servant of Jeroboam" dates it about 775 B.C. (107). The drawing suggests that the craftsman who cut the figure of the lion was a man of no mean skill. The second illustration (108) shows a beautiful seal discovered at Mizpah, which so impressed visitors when it was first unearthed that they arrived in busloads on the site and held up the excavation! Its inscription "Jaazaniah, officer of the king" probably refers to Gedaliah's officer mentioned in II Kings 25. 23; if so, its date would be about 600 B.C. The figure of the fighting cock, with which (so far as we know) the domestic fowl makes its first appearance in Palestine, was probably borrowed from Egypt. Although many of the seal designs were taken from Egypt and Syria, there can be little doubt that for the most part they were executed by native Israelite craftsmen.

Foreign influence is also dominant in the other department of art upon which the excavations have thrown a flood of light— that of interior decorating. We know that Solomon hired Phoenician craftsmen for the building and decorating of his Temple and it is now evident that he was not the only king to patronize foreign artists. In summing up the reign of Ahab of the Northern Kingdom (875–851 B.C.), the writer of I Kings refers to "the ivory house which he built" (22. 39). This was a room in the palace at Samaria which was notable for the ivory inlay of its cedar wall panelling and furniture. By a most remarkable piece of good fortune, the remains of this sumptuous decoration were discovered on the site about twenty years ago and are now known as "the early ivories from Samaria". Most of the ivory pieces **were** shattered into small fragments; some were blackened

108 A fighting cock on a Seal from Mizpah

208

by fire; others, fortunately, were embedded in the clay of disintegrated mud-bricks and so were in a fair state of preservation. On the back of many of the pieces a Hebrew letter had been carved and these are interpreted as guides to the joiner whose job it was to assemble them in the correct order on an article of furniture or on a wall panel. The drawings give us a glimpse into the most famous room of Ahab's palace.

109   A Sphinx in a lotus thicket

Two crouching and open-mouthed lions(9) are the best examples of the small number of ivory pieces carved in the round. We are told that Solomon had lions near the arms and on the steps of his throne (I Kings 10. 19f.) and it is very likely that Ahab followed the same fashion (80). The blank eyes of the lions originally contained some kind of realistic inset (probably of glass), and the inside of their jaws still shows traces of red colouring. The sphinx in a lotus thicket(109) appears to have been part of a border; with its lion's body and human head, it belongs to a category of fabulous creatures which were extremely popular in Egypt at this period. Notice its crown, curling wing and patterned "kilt". Unlike the lions, this piece was carved on a pierced plaque. Other pieces clearly intended as borders were carved in low relief on solid ivory plates. They include stylized but delicate fan-shaped palmettes(7, 110) and interesting knobs, some patterned like the heads of daisies, with

110   Ivory decorations for Panelling and Furniture

209

111   An inlaid Ivory of the Infant Horus

holes in the back for pegs used to fix them in position. The original of the final drawing(111) is a beautiful piece of work from the most spectacular class of the ivories discovered at Samaria. It depicts the infant Horus (an Egyptian god) sitting upon a lotus. On his head is a crown of rams' horns and in his right hand a flail. The surface of the ivory was richly decorated with coloured insets (predominantly blues and greens) and gold-leaf. The workmanship in this type of ivory was extremely delicate, so delicate that the depth of the carving and the ridges between the insets have to be measured in millimetres.

The writer of the authoritative book on these ivories may justly claim that "no other finds have told us so much about the art of the Israelite monarchy".[1] We cannot, however, be certain that they were executed by Israelite craftsmen. The unfinished and unworked ivory found on the site may simply mean that the Syrian workmen visited Samaria to do their work on the spot. What, however, is certain is that the art is characteristically Syrian, despite the use of Egyptian models. The infant Horus, for example, is much plumper than he is in Egyptian versions of the same subject. It is also pointed out that the ivories show no trace of Assyrian influence. Assyrian lions, for example, are shaggy and fierce in appearance, while the lions of the ivories are tame-looking and gracefully carved.

It is not easy to discover how far the wealthy men of Israel followed the fashion of Ahab and indulged in ivory inlay for their panelling and their furniture. Amos in the middle of the eighth century B.C. knew and disapproved of the idle rich who sprawled on "beds of ivory"(6. 4), and about fifty years later we know that worked and unworked ivory was paid as tribute by Hezekiah of Judah to Sennacherib of Assyria. We may take it that ivory decoration was a popular luxury in the circles which could afford such things. One hopes that its artistic merit was as much appreciated as the opportunity it provided for displaying wealth.

[1] J. W. Crowfoot and Grace M. Crowfoot, *Early Ivories from Samaria*, p. 49. Grateful acknowledgment is made for the substance of the foregoing paragraphs and for the excellent photographs from which the drawings were made.

Chapter X

RELIGIOUS LIFE

FOR many people living in twentieth-century Christendom, it is necessary to abandon two deep-rooted assumptions as a first step towards understanding ancient Israel: first, that religion involves (at the very least) the pursuit of truth and goodness; and secondly, that conscious effort is required to relate it to the conditions of everyday life. It may fairly be said that in Old Testament times, Israel suffered not from a lack of religion, but from an excess of it. This does not imply that you can have too much of a good thing; it means, rather, that religion is not necessarily a good thing at all. It is a source of great confusion that this one word is commonly used to describe any and every conception of man's relationship with the Unseen World, whether it is believed to be hostile, capricious, impersonal, immoral, righteous or loving, whether, in fact, you are talking about a base superstition or about the religion of Christ. This wide meaning of religion helps explain why the history of Old Testament times is as much the story of a conflict between different and radically opposed kinds of religion, as it is the story of a conflict between social groups and rival empires.

Two principal kinds of religion competed for the allegiance of the ancient Israelites and the Old Testament is unintelligible without some insight into their different origin and nature. First, there is the religion of the Canaanites, well-established in Palestine before the Israelite Conquest, elaborate in its ritual and thoroughly identified with the interests and pursuits of an agricultural population. Secondly, there is the religion of Moses and the semi-nomads who came out of Egypt and settled in Palestine. This was the very antithesis of the religion they found on their arrival—austere, simply-organized, cradled in a desert rather than a settled society, and, therefore, not in the least geared to the everyday life of men who tilled the soil.

Canaanite religion was identified with Nature and aimed at enabling men to co-operate with and control the cycle of the seasons, whereas the religion of Moses claimed to have stemmed, not from man's desire to be comfortable in and exploit the natural order, but from an act in which God had revealed his nature and sought man's response to his purpose. It rested, that is to say, on the authority of historical revelation. The conflict between these two religions was one of the most momentous struggles in the spiritual history of the world, since on the victory of Moses, the whole future of Judaism and Christianity hinged.

The victory of the faith of Moses was, however, neither immediate nor complete. For many of the Israelites, it was a case of "when in Canaan, do as the Canaanites do"; they did not know, as Hosea pointed out, that it was *their* God, who gave them "the corn, and the wine, and the oil" (2. 8), and so they took over wholesale the cults and sanctuaries of the people of the land. This is not very surprising when it is realized that Canaanite religion was as much a part of their agricultural life as water, gas and electricity are a part of ours. The cult of the sanctuaries was in no sense looked upon as a spiritual luxury for those who happened to fancy that kind of thing, but, rather, as a necessity of life—an indispensable fertilizer without which the growth of the crops and the prosperity of the people were inconceivable. On the other hand, the religion of Moses was not a religion of nature and it provided no recipes for fertility. Its bearing on the new conditions of life in Palestine had to be worked out, just as Christian missionaries have to work out how the faith they introduce to new societies (often proud of their old traditions) may be "naturalized" without being destroyed. This process of acclimatization is obviously one of great delicacy and complexity, and it tends to throw into relief two quite different ways of approaching the problem. First, there is the method of uncompromising rigour towards the established religion, which attempts to wipe out all its sanctuaries and festivals and everything connected with them. As this procedure involves changing not only the religion of the people, but their whole manner of life, it has rarely, if ever, been wholly successful. The second method consists in *adopting* what in the old religion is compatible with the new and *adapting* practices which cannot easily be abolished, but equally cannot be taken over as they stand. The question then becomes one of knowing where to draw the line and the verdict of history has often been that this second approach has sacrificed quality to quantity, the distinctiveness of the new religion for the advantage of gaining adherents.

It is impossible to trace any simple pattern of the interaction of these two methods in the many-sided religion of the Old Testament, but it is not distorting the facts unduly to find in the priestly religion of the sanctuaries much of that adoption and adaptation of Canaanite practices which characterize the second method, and in the faith of the prophets much of that uncompromising and iconoclastic rigour which belongs to the first method. The Old Testament sometimes shows us priests and prophets working together in partnership and sometimes ranged in bitter opposition. Both elements are part of the total picture. Priests and prophets alike laboured to maintain the faith of Moses in a society soaked in the culture of Canaan, although their common purpose tends to be obscured by the diversity of their respective methods. Also, it would be unfair to forget that Israel had hundreds of priests drawn from the rank and file of society, whereas the prophets were picked men. In this respect, they are scarcely comparable. The difficult nature of their common task can hardly be exaggerated. With its art, architecture, music and commerce, the culture of Canaan stood for Progress (with a capital P). The so-called "scientific attitude" of our own day makes, as the Churches well know, a similar kind of popular appeal. By comparison, the stern austerity of the Mosaic tradition appeared stick-in-the-mud and opposed to the spirit of the Modern Age.

It will already be clear that the religion of everyday life represented neither the most distinctive nor the most significant tradition of Israel. In every age, it is at the level of daily practices (especially among peasant populations) that superstitious rituals and old wives' tales retain their hold, long after they have been expressly repudiated by the people's acknowledged religious leaders.

THE RELIGION OF THE CANAANITES

Our knowledge of Canaanite religion has increased almost beyond recognition during the last twenty-five years by the discovery and deciphering of hundreds of clay tablets from a temple library at Ras Shamra, the site of the ancient city of Ugarit, on the north coast of Syria. These religious texts prove conclusively that the opposition with which the Mosaic tradition

213

112 The god of Thunder

had to contend was no mere conglomeration of hole-and-corner fertility cults presided over by petty gods and goddesses, but, rather, one of the most elaborate religious systems of the ancient world.

Among its many deities, the most powerful was Baal, the "Lord of the Earth" and the god of the weather. His voice was the thunder; when he opened the sluices of the clouds, rain fell to give life to the earth. A bas-relief from Ras Shamra, generally thought to represent Baal, shows him brandishing a thunder-bolt in his right hand and lightning in his left (112). It is an interesting experiment to compare this figure with the storm god of Psalm 29; the writer of the psalm, Israelite though he was, might well have been writing a caption for the picture. The second illustration of Baal (113) is taken from a fine bronze statuette (originally covered with gold-leaf), also found at Ras Shamra. The general posture of the figure and the position of the right arm suggest that, as before, he is in the act of hurling a thunderbolt.

Baal is the hero of many Canaanite myths, which were used to accompany and explain elaborate rituals. For the most part, they are concerned with the fertility of the land and the creation of the world in the beginning. Particular importance was attached to the myth of the god's death and resurrection, which were commemorated in annual ceremonies. Baal, as the giver of fertility, was represented as dying when the "latter rains" ceased and the summer sun scorched the earth, and as coming to life again in the autumn. His resurrection caused the "former rains" to fall and launched the agricultural year on another cycle.

The Ras Shamra texts also contain a version of the wide-spread myth of the creation of the world, which represented it as the outcome of a fight in which the god slays the Chaos Monster, depicted as a sea-dragon and often called

113 A graven image of Baal

214

114   The Seven-headed Leviathan

Leviathan (as in Psalm 74. 14). By the victory of the god, Order was brought out of Chaos and the Creation came into being. The cylinder-seal impression (of the kind referred to on pp. 180f.), from which the illustration (114) is taken shows the Chaos Monster in the throes of death. Four of its seven heads have already been overcome. The illustration on p. 181 (also from a cylinder-seal impression) gives another version of the same myth. Here, the figure second from the left, saw in hand, stands on the Dragon of the Deep as its conqueror. This "deep", incidentally, is identical with the "deep" of the first creation story of Genesis (1. 2; compare Isaiah 51. 9f.) and is probably represented by the waves surrounding the god who sits enthroned at the right of the picture.

The rich mythology of Canaanite religion implies an elaborate ritual, and all the evidence shows that it was enacted in sumptuous temples with every aid from art and music. The performance of these rites was the responsibility of a large and highly-organized priesthood under the leadership of a hereditary High Priest. There is no doubt that Canaanite religion was gorgeous and spectacular; there is equally no doubt that it was in the highest degree obscene. In addition to the male members of the pantheon (for Baal by no means stood alone), we hear of the goddesses Anath, Asherah and Astarte, and the myths in which they were actresses make it clear that their principal concerns were sex and fertility. The temples had a special staff to put their repulsive notions into daily practice.

THE LOCAL SANCTUARIES

Every village and town in Israel had its own sanctuary, which served (so to speak) as the parish church of the local community. It was commonly called the "high place" and, as the name suggests, it was often to be found on the top of a hill. Its site, however, was chosen less for the convenience of those who used it than for its sacred associations. As many Israelite sanctuaries were taken over from the Canaanites, they enjoyed a long tradition as holy places, and legends were treasured which recounted how, by a divine appearance, the spot had been marked out as being especially sacred.

The centre-piece of every sanctuary was its altar. Its nature and purpose are succinctly described in an ancient law:

> An altar of earth thou shalt make unto me, and shalt sacrifice thereon thy burnt offerings, and thy peace offerings, thy sheep, and thine oxen. . . . And if thou make me an altar of stone, thou shalt not build it of hewn stones: for if thou lift up thy tool upon it, thou hast polluted it (Exodus 20. 24f.).

We may get some general impression of the importance of the altar in a sanctuary from the very big pre-Israelite "high place" which has been excavated at Megiddo(123). The altar, here, was of immense size (26 feet in diameter and 4½ feet high) and built of rubble and unhewn stone. In the latter respect, it was more orthodox than the burnished copper altar outside Solomon's temple.

In Hebrew the word which is translated as "altar" means simply the place where the slaughtering is done. To the ordinary Israelite, therefore, whose whole approach to God was through sacrificial offerings, it was the most sacred thing on earth. This did not mean that he approached it with fear and trembling, but it did mean that he took good care to cleanse himself from ritual impurity before he went to the sanctuary for worship. Once the ritual requirements had been satisfied, his behaviour at the sanctuary was much less subdued than that of a congregation in a Christian church. He displayed, in fact, no inhibitions whatsoever.

One of the most characteristic sights in ancient Palestine was a sacrificial feast. On some festive occasion, a whole family would climb the hill to their local high place, taking with them baskets of food and (if they could afford it) a lamb or a sheep from the flock. After greetings had been exchanged with the priest in charge, which were, no doubt, elaborate and (by our standards) extremely formal, the father, as head of the family, would take the animal, lay his hand on its head, and then cut its throat. He would be particularly careful to drain every drop of its blood on to the stones of the altar, for blood, upon which life so clearly depended, was charged with mystery and belonged to God alone. The priest would then help him skin and dress the carcase and see that certain special parts of it (notably the fat of the entrails and kidneys) were placed upon the altar and burnt. The rest of the meat would then be cut up, put in a large stew-pot, and set on a fire to boil. Meanwhile, other members of the party would have been making offerings of olive oil and wine (for what was a feast without wine?), pouring a little of each on to the stones of the altar. Such libations, it was believed, sanctified the whole supply. When the mutton was fully cooked, everybody (including the priest) sat down on the ground and began their meal in the open air, picnic fashion. Before darkness fell, the company would be singing and dancing, for in the period before the Exile, to offer a sacrifice was essentially to "rejoice before the Lord".

It is inconceivable that sacrifices were only offered "weather permitting". The great feasts, it is true, all fell in the dry season, but new moons and sabbaths, as well as many private celebrations, continued throughout the winter months. We have no means of knowing, however, what happened to these open-air picnics, when it was pouring with rain. In all probability, the important city sanctuaries had buildings like the temples of the Canaanites and these, presumably, contained dining-rooms, as well as chambers for the priest and his sacred treasures. Even, however, at enclosed sanctuaries, the altar remained outside the building, for reasons which became increasingly obvious, when, in the course of time, whole burnt offerings gained in popularity. In this type of sacrifice, the complete carcase of the animal was burnt on the altar and went up in smoke. On such an occasion, there was, of course, no meal.

The open-air sanctuary of the village, simple though it was, consisted of more than an altar in a sacred enclosure. We hear, for example, a good deal about the "pillars" of the high places, which the prophets and lawgivers always castigate as foreign abominations. These stone obelisks, which were anything up to about ten feet in height, had for centuries been a familiar feature of Canaanite sanctuaries. Their precise significance is difficult to determine. Some scholars have suggested that they were intended for libations in some cult of the dead and others regard them as being little more than monuments of the presence of deity—like Jacob's pillar at Bethel (Genesis 28. 16–22). It is more than likely that they were eventually shaped into idols.

Coupled with these pillars, the Old Testament writers often mention the "Asherim" (for example, II Kings 17. 10), of which "Asherah" is the singular form. This is another puzzling borrowing from the Canaanites. As we have seen, they had a fertility goddess called Asherah and there is no doubt that she had been given a place in popular Israelite religion. The puzzle arises from the fact that the "Asherim" are described as things which could be cut down, burned and planted. The most probable conclusion to be drawn from this mixed evidence is that they were either wooden images of the goddess Asherah or poles and trees symbolic of her worship. It is not impossible that they were regarded as the female element in a fertility cult and that the stone pillars symbolized the male element, but this is a speculation which cannot be proved. The very presence of Asherah, however, arouses one's worst suspicions.

The sanctuaries of Dan and Bethel, which were established in the Northern Kingdom as rivals to Jerusalem, were notorious for possessing "golden calves" (I Kings 12. 25–30). Recent investigations, however, have suggested the improbability of their having been idols in the ordinary sense of directly representing God as a bull. It is much more likely that the calves were thought of as animals on which the invisible deity rode or stood, just as in the Jerusalem Temple, he was conceived of as being enthroned on two winged sphinxes or "cherubim" (see pp. 226f.). Nevertheless, the association of the God of Israel in any way with so obvious a Canaanite symbol of fertility as the bull(119) was dangerous and disastrous.

The only other major piece of equipment in the local sanctuary was either a spring, or failing that, an artificial water cistern. As worship involved processes we normally associate with the kitchen, water was obviously a practical necessity, but in the mind of the Israelite its real importance was symbolic. We shall not be far wrong if we associate it with the waters of the Great

218

115 Canaanite captives in Egypt about 1200 B.C. (*see p.* 90)

116 A Potter at his Wheel: a limestone figure of about 2500 B.C. from an Egyptian tomb (*see p.* 129)

117 A pillar-base figurine
     (*see p*. 232)

118 Terracotta model of horse with
     sun hat (*see p*. 80)

119 (*left*) Bull vase from Cyprus and (*right*) an imitation found at Jerusalem

Deep, as it is found depicted, for example, on the seal impression of the Creation myth from Uz(86).

The guardian of the sanctuary was the local priest and he clearly held an important position in the life of the community. It is very probable that the office was handed down from father to son and usually remained in the same family for generations. Contrary to the popular idea of his work, the priest was much more the guardian and teacher of religious tradition than a minister of sacrificial worship. As we have seen, he was little more than an assistant when offerings were being made at the altar. His chief job was to work the sacred oracle, that is, to supply answers to difficult questions by divining the will of God. The basic principle of the oracle is clear enough; it was simply a mechanism which said "yes" or "no" to a question stated in a form which admitted of that kind of answer. But what exactly the mechanism was remains completely obscure. We hear, for example, of the oracle called "Urim and Thummim", which some have suggested was a marked pebble, used in much the same way as we toss a coin for "heads" or "tails". This, however, is only one of innumerable guesses and is no more likely to be correct than the others. The "ephod", another piece of priestly equipment used in divination, is equally enigmatic. Sometimes the context in which it is mentioned suggests an image and at other times a garment; present opinion tends to favour the latter. Whatever the apparatus used in divination, the decisions announced by the priest were accepted as the will of God and, as such, binding. From these crude and mechanical beginnings, aided no doubt by common sense and more spiritual forms of exercise, the priests of the sanctuaries built up a body of religious law which played no small part in the life of the people.

Associated with the priests were the sanctuary prophets. We know that Canaanite prophets were organized in guilds centred on the larger sanctuaries, as, for example, "the prophets of Baal four hundred and fifty, and the prophets of the Asherah four hundred", with whom Elijah had memorable dealings on Mount Carmel (I Kings 18). Similarly, Israelite cultic prophets were to be found in and around the sanctuaries, roving about in rowdy troops, working themselves up into frenzies by dancing and music, and uttering semi-coherent oracles which the credulous accepted as divinely inspired. We may readily sympathize with Amos, who strenuously rejected the suggestion that he was one of these "sons of the prophets" (7. 14). In Old Testament times, it is always wise to remember, there were prophets *and prophets*.

THE TEMPLE OF SOLOMON

The most famous sanctuary of Israel was the temple which Solomon built at Jerusalem(120). In Old Testament times, the Jerusalem Temple had not yet become the only legitimate centre of Jewish worship, but as the "royal chapel" of the capital, it inevitably assumed a high degree of importance in the people's religious life. Solomon entrusted its design and construction to Phoenician craftsmen and nothing could better demonstrate the way in which the ambitions of the monarchy stimulated the adoption of Canaanite culture and Canaanite religious ideas. Recent reconstructions, which interpret the descriptions of I Kings 6 and Ezekiel 41 in the light of a considerable body of new archaeological evidence,[1] represent it as a typical Canaanite temple, both in its general architectural design and in many of its interior decorations and fittings. Despite the fact that the Queen of Sheba found it breath-taking, it was far from setting an example of authentic Israelite worship to the whole land. It is not surprising that when the Babylonians burnt it to the ground in 586 B.C., the prophet Jeremiah took the view that true religion could continue without it. It is worth, however, a rapid conducted tour.

Let us imagine, therefore, that we are visitors to Jerusalem about the year 930 B.C. and that we are in the extremely fortunate position of having obtained permission to go round the temple, despite the regulation which puts it out of bounds to all but the king and his priests.

We make our approach from the east, with the valley of the Kidron behind us, and as we enter the outer court, we notice a number of small buildings in the corners to the left and the right. Our guide tells us that they are only annexes and have no merit to make them worth pausing over. It is certainly the temple itself which holds the eye, with its white limestone, already weathered in places to a pleasant pink, gleaming in the brilliant sunshine. One could not call it a magnificent building;

---

[1] Excellent summaries may be found in articles by G. Ernest Wright and Paul L. Garber in *The Biblical Archaeologist* for May 1941 and February 1951, to both of which the following paragraphs are deeply indebted.

120 The Temple of Solomon from the east. Notice its crenellated battlement, free standing columns and slit-windows. There was a porch between the outer entrance and the decorated doors, but this is not clearly seen in the drawing

in size, it is more like a parish church or even a college chapel than an English Cathedral (we did rather expect it to be the Hebrew Westminster Abbey). Our guide (who is as fond of statistical measurements as the book of Kings) dutifully informs us that the whole building, from end to end, is not much more than 100 feet long. Its roof is, of course, flat and its peculiarly modern and symmetrical appearance (rather like a cinema) is relieved only by a range of low buildings which run round the whole structure (except the front) in a way reminiscent of the side aisles of a church. Above the flat roof of these side-chambers (for that is what the low buildings prove to be) are small windows set in the middle of each side of the building. The whole chapel is set on a platform of solid blocks of stone, leaving space round the edge wide enough to walk on comfortably and raising the floor of the building about 9 feet from the level of the court.

As we come nearer, two great objects in the court attract our attention. On the left, there is a huge bronze basin, resting on twelve bronze bull-calves arranged in groups of three, each group facing a point of the compass. Our guide tells us that this is known as the "Molten Sea" and he would have us believe that it is capable of holding something like 10,000 gallons of water. As it stands over 7 feet high, it is impossible to see

121 The Altar of Burnt Offering which stood in front of Solomon's
Temple (*as described in Ezekiel 43. 13–17*)

inside, but we are given to understand that the metal is about
3 inches thick and that the whole apparatus weighs between
25 and 30 tons. It is difficult to know whether to admire the
metal workers who cast it and brought it in one piece to its
present site, or our guide for the plausible way in which he
induces us to accept his weights and measurements. Nevertheless, it is a large and magnificent basin, grand enough to
symbolize the Great Deep.

Hardly less remarkable is the burnished copper object on
our right—the Altar of Burnt Offering. It looks like a miniature
Babylonian *ziggurat*, built in three stages on a square base (121).
This, we are told, is the altar on which parts of the sacrificial
victims are burned by the priests. It is not difficult to picture
worshippers gathered round in groups, gazing up to the point
at which, 15 feet above the ground, the sacrificial smoke rose
heavenwards.

Turning now to the main building, we can examine what we
are tempted to call the "west end" (actually, it is the *east* end of
the building we are looking at, but the "sanctuary" is at the
opposite end). It is entirely dominated by two huge burnished
bronze pillars, which tower above the roof level of the side-
chambers and (according to your guide) are not much short of
40 feet in height and 18 feet in circumference. They are unusual
in every way, but chiefly for the fact that they have names; the

224

one on the right is called *Jachin* and the one on the left *Boaz*. No entirely satisfactory explanation of these names is forthcoming, but it is probable that they represent the opening words of inscriptions or formulae invoking the divine protection on the building. It is impossible to inspect in detail the elaborate capitals of these two columns, but they are richly decorated with lilies and festooned with hundreds of small metal pomegranates. We are told that the really important feature to notice is that the pillars are free-standing and do not support any part of the building.

A flight of steps brings us up to the level of the platform and to the entrance of the Porch. Passing through this entrance (it is without doors), we find ourselves in a small and simple chamber, with a kind of parquet floor made of cypress, but without either windows or furniture. Our attention is entirely taken by the tall double-doors ahead of us, which are heavily decorated with flowers, palm-trees, and winged animals. These carvings are all inlaid with gold and look absolutely magnificent in the sunlight. Going through the doors, we come to the first of the two rooms which form the main structure of the building.

The simple chamber we have just left is called *Elam* (or Porch), and the two inner rooms, in the order in which we reach them are called *Hekal* (or Holy Place) and *Debir* (or Holy of Holies)(122). It is immediately clear that we have now arrived at the biggest room of the Temple. The Holy Place, as it is called, is 60 feet long, 30 feet wide and 45 feet high. Shafts of light stream down through latticed windows high up the side walls, giving us the general impression of a clerestory. Unlike the Porch, the Holy Place is decorated and includes a little furniture. The walls are panelled in cedar and divided at regular intervals by pilasters in the form of stylized palm-trees (symbolizing the Tree of Life) and each of them is "guarded" by two

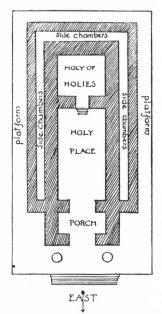

122 The Temple of Solomon

225

sphinx-like creatures carved on the lower part of the panels. The pilasters rise almost to the ceiling, which is supported on huge cedar beams. There is a small door in each of the two side walls and we are told that these lead to the side-chambers, which we shall have time to visit briefly on the way out. For the moment, the furnishings of the room must have our attention. The most elegant objects are ten tall and slender gold lamp-stands, each with a bowl at the top in which seven wicks are burning(26). There is also a small table, called the table of shewbread, on which unleavened cakes are laid by the priests and changed at regular intervals. The only other object is small but striking in appearance—a gold-plated stand about $4\frac{1}{2}$ feet high and 3 feet square, which, we are informed, is the altar of incense(63). It is this and the cedar panelling which accounts for the pleasant smell in the building—so different from what we feared and imagined on first learning about animal sacrifice!

At the end of the Holy Place, a flight of steps leads up to the doors of the Holy of Holies. These are made of a beautiful light olive-wood and as we push them open they swing right back on special door-posts (pentagonal in section) and reveal the *Debir*, the temple's most holy chamber. Perhaps "reveal" is scarcely the right word, for it is very difficult to see anything at all at first since the only light in the room is that which comes through the doorway we have just passed. As soon as our eyes get used to the dimness, we can make out two enormous figures facing us, each 15 feet high with two out-stretched wings $7\frac{1}{2}$ feet long. The outside wings nearly touch the walls of the room and the inside wings seem to touch in the middle. On closer inspection we discover that they are larger models of the sphinxes we have seen already on the doors and the panelling; they are, we are told, the Cherubim. It seems that we must give up for ever the idea that a cherub is a pink chubby-faced baby with tiny wings. This notion has nothing to do with the Hebrews and was introduced by Renaissance artists drawing on Greek models. It is now known that ancient kings were depicted as sitting on "cherub thrones"(80), that is, on thrones supported on each side by a winged animal, like a lion, with a human head, and this gives us the clue to what a cherub really looked like(124) and meant to the Israelites. When the Old Testament speaks of God as one who "sitteth upon the cherubim" (I Samuel 4. 4), we are to think, therefore, of God

226

enthroned as king. The difference between the Israelite and Canaanite ideas on the subject is apparent in the Holy of Holies, for here there is no image of God. His glory was invisible and was thought of as being borne on the outstretched wings.

The only other object in the Holy of Holies is the Ark of the Covenant, which rests on the floor in the centre beneath the wing-tips of the two cherubim. To the casual visitor, it seems to be no more than a small wooden box with a hinged lid and two carrying poles. The devout Israelite, however, believed that it contained the stone tables of the Law and that its golden lid was the Mercy Seat.

Before leaving the Holy of Holies, it is worth pausing over the dimensions of the room. It is an exact cube—30 feet wide, 30 feet long and 30 feet high. To achieve this regularity, the builders not only raised the floor level (as we noticed when we came up the stairs from the Holy Place), but also lowered the ceiling. In order to avoid breaking the line of the roof outside, a false roof was constructed inside and suspended with great skill.

As we make our way out, we pay our promised visit to the side-chambers. We obtain access through one of the two doors in the north and south walls of the Holy Place and ascend a winding stair to the top floor. In all, there are three stories in the side buildings and it is curious that the size of the rooms increases slightly as you move from the ground floor to the top. A corridor runs round three sides of the main building at each level and has connecting doors to a string of rooms which look very much like offices. There isn't time to go into any of them, but we are told that they serve the same purpose as the vestries

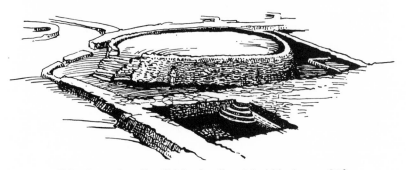

123   A pre-Israelite "high place" at Megiddo (*see p.* 216)

124 One of the Cherubim

of churches and the muniment rooms of cathedrals. They are used, that is to say, by the temple officials as store-rooms—for vestments, treasures, records and miscellaneous equipment required for worship.

We return by the same winding stairs, pass through the Holy Place and the Porch. Standing between *Jachin* and *Boaz*, we have our final view of the temple court. Over the "Molten Sea", it is just possible to see the roof-tops of Solomon's palace, which though built at a lower level was essentially part of the same plan. It is strange to think that the Phoenician craftsmen spent twice as long on their house for the king of Israel as they did on the house for the King of Heaven. Solomon paid the piper; presumably, he called the tune.

THE GREAT FESTIVALS

Before the Exile, the Israelites had three great annual festivals and they were all connected with the life of the farming community. Although trade, industry and commerce were expanding rapidly, they have left no trace in the religious records. We can hardly criticize this omission, when even today, it is still seedtime and harvest, rather than occasions like "Industrial Sunday", which loom large in popular religious sentiment.

The first feast of the year was *Passover*, or the *Feast of Unleavened Bread*. Its double name suggests a composite origin and the elements of which it is composed turn out, on examination, to be very complicated indeed. All we need notice is that two of the celebrations which have gone to the making of the feast belong to the world of the farmer and stockbreeder. The older is a lambing festival from Israel's nomadic days, which at an early date was connected with the Exodus from Egypt and thereafter celebrated to commemorate the Israelites' deliverance (see pp. 31f.). The more recent is a Canaanite feast of the barley harvest, when unleavened cakes were eaten. These two spring festivals were combined, with the result that the historical commemoration of the Exodus (the Passover) entirely eclipsed their original meaning for the shepherd and the farmer. It is a telling example of the victory of the religion of Moses over the religion of Canaan. It is impossible to be certain when the two were combined, but it is likely that the Canaanite feast at the beginning of the barley harvest was observed more or less in its old form for the greater part of Old Testament times.

The second festival of the year, the *Feast of Weeks*, always remained a purely agricultural celebration. It was held in summer at the beginning of the wheat harvest, which (at least in theory) followed seven weeks after the cutting of the first stalks of barley. If we disregard the formal regulations of the law codes, which transfer the feast to the Jerusalem Temple from its natural setting on the farms and in the villages, the picture which emerges is comparatively simple. When the wheat was ripe, the head of each farming family cut enough of the crop for two or three sheaves(125) and he and his sons took them to the local sanctuary. Here they were ceremonially presented to God. We may guess (for evidence on the point is lacking) that either the party took the priest back home for a festal meal, or else they sacrificed an animal at the sanctuary and made their feast there.

The *Feast of Ingathering*, held in the autumn, so far outshone the other two as to be called quite simply "the Feast". Here we find Israel's most extensive borrowing from Canaanite religion and, in consequence, the greatest degree of reticence in the orthodox law books. There was, indeed, much to keep dark. The law books agree, however, that those taking part should forsake their houses for the period of the celebration and dwell in booths and it is implied that these booths should be made of branches cut down from trees. It is from this provision that the festival gets its alternative name—the "Feast of Tabernacles" (or "Booths"). The booths and the branches in the Jerusalem celebrations are a pale reflection of the hilarious days spent in the vineyards when the grapes and the olives were being gathered in (see pp. 104–8). Despite the orthodox interpretation it received later, everything suggests that throughout this period, the festival was an occasion when the whole population let themselves go in the wildest revelry. Its dominant theme was Nature's fertility and, as is only too obvious from Canaanite sources, this easily degenerated into plain debauchery. We are almost completely in the dark about the connexion of this feast with the orthodox sanctuary and

125   Reaping the first-fruits of the
Wheat Harvest

the distinctive Israelite tradition. It has been suggested that in the Jerusalem Temple, where, of course, it was cut off from its intimate connexion with the vintage, the autumn festival took on much more the character of a New Year celebration. The leading role, it is surmised, was played by the reigning king, through whom God's blessing was guaranteed for another year. Whatever the exact nature of this final festival at the "turn of the year", we may be confident that both in the capital and in the countryside, its rites combined thanksgiving for the in-gathered harvest and petition for the coming seedtime.

EVERYDAY RELIGION

The three great festivals no more exhausted the Israelite's religious life than do Christmas, Easter and Whitsuntide that of the Christian. Indeed, it is evident that the average Israelite was to be found at his local sanctuary more often than the average Christian at his local church.

There was in Israel a deep sense that life was not something to be taken for granted. Men and nature were dependent on God (in a way which our push-button age has forgotten) and without his continued blessing, it was believed, they would surely perish. It was for this reason that the first-fruits of the crops and the first-born of the flocks were regularly brought to the sanctuary and offered sacrificially. By origin and right, the *whole* crop and the *whole* flock were his and it was to represent the whole that a part was given up. Man could use the rest for his own purposes only after this acknowledgement had been made. We are, therefore, to imagine a constant succession of private harvest festivals at the sanctuary, when individual farmers brought sheaves of barley and wheat, newly-threshed grain, the first loaf of bread baked from the season's crop, baskets of olives and grapes, and the first skins of wine and oil.

The shepherd, too, in season would bring his first lamb and his first fleece. We do not know precisely what form these various offerings took, but a liturgy for the offering of summer fruits in Deuteronomy 26. 1–11 shows that at least in Jerusalem it was accompanied by prayer and the reciting of a kind of creed. No doubt the ceremony was simpler in the village sanctuaries and the priest was able to live on the people's offerings even in the days before they were formally fixed as "tenths" or "tithes".

In Canaanite religion, the idea of offering the first-fruits and the first-born did not stop short of the first-born of men. Israel's laws recognized child sacrifice in theory (Exodus 22. 29), but shrank from it in practice (Exodus 34. 20). Among the masses of the people, who were most deeply influenced by the old religion of the land, the revolting custom was not entirely abandoned, as we may learn from the vigorous protests of the law and the prophets.

To examine all the occasions when the Israelite visited his sanctuary would be to pass under review almost the whole of his daily life. He went when he was sick, either for a diagnosis or a cure. He went to be certified as ritually clean after various kinds of physical disorder, or after he had been away in the wars. He went to establish his innocence of crimes of which he was accused and perhaps even to have his enemies cursed in a priestly ritual. He went to make lamentation in distress, vows in need, and thanksgiving in prosperity. The taunt made against "four-wheeler" Christians, who go to church only in a perambulator, a taxi and a hearse (for baptism, for marriage and for burial) certainly could not be transferred to the average Israelite!

The prophets were singularly unimpressed by all this religious busyness. They asserted that the people had abandoned the true God for heathen idolatries and that their much-frequented sanctuaries were sinks of iniquity. Recent archaeological discoveries go a long way towards confirming their condemnation of popular religion. It is significant, for example, that on the ostraca from eighth-century Samaria (see pp. 182 f.), the proportion of names compounded with Baal suggests that no less than a third of the population practised some form of Canaanite religion. Evidence from Judah, on the other hand, suggests a higher standard of loyalty to the religion of Moses, but more than one foreign cult was to be found even in the Jerusalem Temple. Ezekiel was particularly aghast at the sun worship

231

there and a Canaanite fertility cult, which he calls "weeping for Tammuz" (8. 14).

The Tammuz cult in the temple was being practised by women, and it appears that they must bear their full share of responsibility for introducing heathen practices into Israel. For example, as Jeremiah protested, they were worshipping the Queen of Heaven (the Canaanite goddess Astarte) at small incense altars in the streets of Jerusalem (63). To the bad record of the women may be added the activities of Solomon's wives, who imported the worship of the gods of Moab and Ammon, and of Jezebel, the wife of Ahab, who brought with her from Phoenicia the cult of the Tyrian Baal.

The female figurines, many of which have been excavated, were also popular with women, but they are rather less serious. The specimen from Lachish in the photograph (117) shows the Mother Goddess looking more pleasant than usual, although when she had her cheeks painted red, she must have appeared distinctly garish. We cannot be certain that pottery figures like this were treated as idols; it is thought much more probable that they were kept in houses as lucky charms. It is not impossible, however, that the prophets reckoned them with the "teraphim" (I Samuel 15. 23) and these certainly earn their condemnation. In the story of Rachel and Laban, the "teraphim" are explicitly household gods, the possession of which symbolizes leadership of the family (Genesis 31. 30). They were undoubtedly small idols, like the creature unearthed at Nuzi (126).

THE FAITH OF THE PROPHETS

The prophetic tradition of Israel is rather like an iceberg in the sense that only the summit of it ever sees the light. From about the middle of the eighth century B.C., we begin to meet men like Amos, Hosea, Isaiah, Micah and Jeremiah, whose personalities are distinctive, but whose message bears the stamp of a common conviction. If we take seriously their claim to speak in the name and with the authority of God, the unity of their message will cause us no surprise. Nor, if we take seriously their claim that it was God who called Israel into being (making a people out of a lot of disunited tribesmen), shall we be surprised

126 One of the Teraphim

232

that the constant burden of their preaching was the need to recover the religious loyalty they knew at the beginning, before they entered the land of Canaan. They look back to Moses as the first of their line, but between him and Amos, it is difficult to trace the prophetic tradition; spasmodic narratives, like those of Samuel and Elijah are enough to prove, however, that the succession was never broken. The faith of Moses was, no doubt, also kept alive by other religious leaders, including faithful priests, who resisted the seductive influence of the Canaanite cults. It is indeed a very remarkable fact that, despite the disgusting superstitions embraced by the masses of the people, there was always an official religion in Israel, which insisted on the worship of the One God, who was not to be represented under any form of graven image and who demanded righteous conduct. Israel never ceased to be a distinctive people.

Although the distinctive vocation of Israel was the theme of the prophets' preaching, they did not win their place in the spiritual history of the world by mouthing pulpit platitudes. No teachers were ever more concrete; no preachers ever more direct. That is why you can go a long way towards reconstructing everyday life in Old Testament times from their sermons alone. No theme is too big for them, no detail too small. Racketeers in the markets, kings in their palaces, corrupt judges at the gates; callous cruelty and licentious luxury in the houses of the rich and powerful; sordid immorality and idolatry in the sanctuaries—all are picked out and shot down. Although the prophets were acutely sensitive to social evils, they were more than sociologists; their diagnosis went to the root of the matter and they called it bluntly the repudiation of God. Because they saw that Israel's failure was (as we should say) religious, they saved their sharpest barbs for the degenerate popular cults.

The vital difference between the faith of the prophets and the everyday religion of the sanctuaries was to be found in the prophets' awareness of God as *personal* and, therefore, akin to, but transcending, man's highest human experience. Such a conception entirely precluded the cajolery and clamour with which the masses tried to get their way with their gods. These gods required handling with care and their priests possessed the "know-how". On the other hand, the Lord of the prophets demanded that men should do justly, and love mercy and walk humbly with their God. Between these two conceptions of religion, there is a deep gulf fixed.

When men did unjustly, hated mercy and rebelled against their God, they brought judgement upon themselves. The prophets did not hesitate, with a confidence which we may well find strange, to interpret the Assyrian and Babylonian wars against Israel as the working out of God's righteous purpose. The devastation of Jerusalem and the deportation of its leading citizens to exile in Babylon was to them the climax of judgement on a disobedient people. Such a stern message of doom was demanded by the prophets' times, but their fundamental faith demanded with equal insistence that this should not be the last word.

Despite her unworthiness, Israel could not be finally obliterated, because she had a place in God's purpose. The prophets believed, therefore, that He would recreate her to be His servant in the world. This is the faith which inspired Judaism after the Exile and it underlies the many different ways in which her religious leaders coupled Israel's mission with God's achievement of His final goal. They called it the coming of the Kingdom. Already on the threshold of the Exile, Jeremiah, the greatest of the goodly fellowship, had declared his certainty of the outcome and described the quality of that true religion which would be realized in the end: "I will put my law in their inward parts, and in their heart will I write it; and I will be their God, and they shall be my people." When the first Christians made these words their own and proclaimed that Jeremiah's New Covenant had indeed been established with the coming of Christ, they placed themselves in the tradition of Israel's prophetic faith and endowed it with the highest possible significance.

INDEX

The numerals in heavy type refer to the *figure numbers* of the illustrations

INDEX

INDEX

INDEX

239

INDEX

240